Robert F. Kennedy

SERIES EDITOR: BARBARA LEAH ELLIS

KONSTANTIN SIDORENKO

Robert F. Kennedy

A Spiritual Biography

A Crossroad 8th Avenue Book
The Crossroad Publishing Company
New York

The Crossroad Publishing Company
481 Eighth Avenue, Suite 1550
New York, NY 10001

First published in 2000 by The Crossroad Publishing Company

Copyright © 2000 by Konstantin Sidorenko

LIBRARY OF CONGRESS CATALOGING-IN-PUBLICATION DATA
Sidorenko, Konstantin, 1956–
Robert F. Kennedy: a spiritual biography / by Konstantin Sidorenko
p. cm.
Includes bibliographical references and index.
ISBN 0-8245-2355-5
1. Kennedy, Robert F., 1925-1968. 2. Kennedy, Robert F.,
1925-1968—Religion. 3. Legislators—United States—Biography.
4. United States. Congress. Senate—Biography. I. Title.
E840.8.K4 S57   2000
973.922'092—dc21
[B]   00-010621

Printed in the United States of America
Set in Janson
Designed and produced by SCRIBES Editorial
Cover design by Kaeser and Wilson Design Ltd.

1 2 3 4 5 6 7 8 9 10 04 03 02 01 00

to Maggie

CONTENTS

Robert F. Kennedy

Senator Robert F. Kennedy, 1967.
(© *The New York Times*)

1

Man of Myths

Multitudes, multitudes in the valley of decision:
for the day of the Lord is near in the valley of decision.

—Joel 3:14

A BARBER ARRIVED AT THE Hickory Hill home of Senator Robert F. Kennedy on Saturday around 8 a.m. Senator Edward M. Kennedy, opposed but resigned to his brother's decision, gave instructions that the hair should be cut as short as possible; not to pay any attention to the wishes of the soon-to-be-official candidate for president. "Cut off as much as you can," he instructed as the barber went up the stairs.

David Burke, chief aid to Edward, came downstairs after the barber and confirmed the candidate was getting his hair cut. Ethel Kennedy had been helping her husband get dressed. The candidate would be wearing a blue suit and a narrow red and blue tie, the tie clasped with a PT-109 pin, a memento of his brother Jack's war exploits. She had nine others, her children, to get ready for the event, too. Eleven-month-old Douglas Harriman, their tenth child, would stay at home with the nurse. (Ethel would give birth to their eleventh child in December). Theodore Sorensen was there that morning, as were Walter J. vanden Heuval and Arthur M. Schlesinger Jr., writers, advisors, historians and friends of the Kennedys.

They all gathered to be with Robert Kennedy during the most important press conference of his life.

"I can't believe it. It is too incredible," Edward had said earlier that morning. "I just can't believe we are sitting around the table discussing anything as incredible as this."[1]

Robert would use a senate caucus room for his 10 a.m. announcement. The room was special to him. From that same room John Fitzgerald Kennedy announced his candidacy for president eight years before. That was also the room Robert first made a name for himself as counsel during the Army-McCarthy hearings in the 1950s and where he faced Jimmy Hoffa, other corrupt union officials and gangsters. Built in 1909, the room was designed to hold 300 people. On March 16, 1968 it held 450 people to hear the words: "I am announcing my candidacy for the president of the United States."

With those words, Robert Kennedy ended months of personal turmoil and public speculation. He knew as he spoke he was breaking one of the cardinal rules of running for president: Do not challenge the re-election of a president of your own party, especially a popular one. President Lyndon B. Johnson was elected four years before by a landslide, beating Arizona Senator Barry Goldwater by sixty-one percent to thirty-nine percent, with Johnson winning all but six states. No serious candidate wanted to challenge such a popular president. Bobby's chances of winning were uncertain. Even if he won the nomination, he might leave enough bitterness within the ranks of the Democratic Party to split it and hand the election over to the Republicans. In any other year except for 1968, Robert Kennedy would have waited since he was the leading candidate, by the reckoning of most political observers, to succeed Johnson in the next election.

Traditional campaign wisdom did not apply in 1968. As he answered questions, Bobby knew Johnson's was a presidency crippled by the war in Vietnam, which split a country becoming increasingly aware its war could not be won. Senator Eugene McCarthy, an anti-war candidate, had nearly beaten Johnson earlier that week in the New Hampshire primary, thus embarrassing a once-popular, sitting president. If Bobby was going to enter the race, he would have to do it soon, before the anti-war, anti-Johnson forces solidified around the newly-serious McCarthy challenge. There were other, more personal factors on his mind as he finished taking questions and got ready to board a plane to fly to New York City.

Robert Kennedy truly believed he was the only candidate politically capable of ending the war. He did not believe McCarthy would make a good president. While trying to find a credible rationalization for his running, he said the country could not survive another four years with Johnson as president. He also worried that the support that still lingered from Jack Kennedy's administration would only ebb if he waited four more years to run. And there was his undeniable personal ambition.

Robert Kennedy, deep in his heart, wanted to be president, thought he deserved to be president and believed he would be president if he worked hard enough. Kennedy very much believed in being part of the action and passion of his times. He did not want to be judged, as Oliver Wendell Holmes put it, as not to have lived. The presidency is the ultimate goal for a politician with such ambitions.

Politics is the art of the possible. No one believed in that statement more than Robert Kennedy, a pragmatist's pragmatist. He did not lead people into lost causes. When he acted, he did not do so recklessly. Despite running against all the rules—not having the open support of most of the country's Democratic power brokers—he saw one chance worth taking. A 1968 candidacy meant that he could count only on his popularity, his celebrity, to win the nomination. Only by showing he had enough popular support could he convince, force, the Democratic Party to nominate him. That was the possibility that convinced him to join the race. But this time when he took the plunge, neither his older brothers nor his father would be there.

Like many of his actions throughout his life, Kennedy's decision to run confirmed both the beliefs of those who endorsed and those who despised him. Even Robert's supporters were still divided about his running in 1968. Months of meetings had failed to convince those hard-nosed political advocates of waiting with those who thought that waiting would mean an opportunity forever lost. His decision to enter the race at that moment showed him for what his opponents thought he had been all along—a ruthless, political opportunist.

If Kennedy were strictly an opportunist, one could not have found a more amateur one. In that first official week of the campaign, he had no campaign staff, headquarters or party support. Many of the people he normally would have counted on to join his effort had been working for Johnson since he became president. Others had gone off to join McCarthy while Kennedy was going through his season of ambivalence. Democratic Party leaders were against his campaign. Of course he still had enough supporters and money to change this around quickly, but nothing like an orchestrated movement to elect Kennedy existed.

The decision was very much in the style of Robert Kennedy: quickly size up the situation, make a decision and plunge in head first. Running for president was for Kennedy not so much cynically seizing the opportunity as it was fulfilling an undeniable urge. Still, he adhered to the politics of the possible. Kennedy was not a dreamer. He believed politics to be a noble profession that could make a difference, but not in the abstract. He reacted to immediate, concrete problems. There was no grand political philosophy from which policies would be drawn in Kennedy's mind. If one policy proved not to work, try another and another until one that worked could be found. The greatest sin was to do nothing.

Robert F. Kennedy came of age several times in what was a long political career during a short life. His life seemed more a series of adolescences, maturing with each campaign, appointment and election. Some parts of his character remained firm at every stage. He was unselfconsciously religious and remained a devout Roman Catholic throughout his life. Even at the most tragic moments, when he could have without fear of criticism drawn a measure of doubt, he remained a true believer in a universe held to order by an omniscient and loving god. His belief in the strength of family was constant. The young Kennedy was a rigid, difficult man, seeing the world in simple terms. He had a black and white vision early on that failed to understand the richness of individual experience. Even his brother John, during his first campaign for congress in 1946, could not see his brother's "silent, sober face" helping him win votes.

John was wrong. Soon, a strong bond would develop between John and Robert. Through the experience of his older, more worldly brother, Robert matured. In stages, his better aspects would emerge. When, at the nadir of his presidency, John found his advisors failing and deceiving him, he turned to the only one he could trust, his brother.

Kennedy would have been seventy-five years old at the start of the twenty-first century had he survived. Those born before the late 1950s will be the last to have direct memories of him; the last ones who remember his presidential campaign, and his murder. He is slowly fading into the exclusive possession of history. The history so far has laminated his life with so many mistakes, fabrications and

Senator Kennedy with Caesar Chavez in 1968.
(© Black Star)

bizarre notions, most of the future historian's time will be spent stripping away the ugly mess before getting to the core material. He has become a man of many myths, romanticized by those who loved him and by those who believe he should be despised.

Some make of the man more than he was, promoting the poetic aura of the martyred leader. People often cite what could have been. Others mock that reaction, preferring instead to criticize the romantic myths that have grown up around Robert Kennedy. Kennedy himself would had disdained such "could have, would have, should have" analysis.

More than most political figures, Robert Kennedy is a Rashomon man. The many labels affixed to his life tell us more about the labeler than the labeled. Was he a newly-minted liberal transformed by his brother's murder, ready to battle for the rights of the poor and downtrodden, or was he the cold-blooded, ruthless politician, ready and willing to trash his beliefs to attain power and glory? The question itself stereotypes the man and gives little insight about him or his times. Even the middle ground that concedes aspects of both the "bad" Bobby and the "good" Bobby can be seen as a conceit of the compromiser.

Does the "Rashomon effect" mean that we can never know the truth about anyone outside our own point of view? Not exactly. The historian's first job is to provide us information on actual deeds. That is the hard work, but the only work worth doing. When the chips were down, what did the politician do? Did he support or denounce a rogue United States senator? Did this politician introduce and work for the passage of a particular bill and did it pass? Did he send in federal troops to allow a single black man to register for a segregated school? Did this politician support a war? These questions might have nuanced explanations, but they can be answered. From there we can decide the legacy of our political figures for ourselves.

Kennedy's popular image is ideal for dual icon on a coin. One side shows the hard-driven, ruthless prosecutor, battering witnesses, ignoring their civil rights. The other side shows his absolute belief in God, the side that gave him faith in himself and an undeniable sympathy for the poor and disadvantaged. Bobby's story is about how he reconciled these opposite forces. Current attacks on RFK ignore his spirituality or conclude it a ruse for personal gain. This view romanticizes Robert Kennedy, too, layering over him an unwarranted venality. Behind the myths is the story of how Robert Kennedy mixed his faith and ambitions. "If his heart was in the hills, his head was in the councils of state," wrote Arthur Schlesinger Jr., RFK's sympathetic and most exhaustive biographer. Schlesinger believes what drove Kennedy more than his personal ends was his devotion to public responsibility.

He was as tough a politician as anyone of his time. He knew as much and more than most about how the country is run. On the other side of his divided nature was the romantic. Much of the criticism of Kennedy points out the differences between the rhetoric and the highly pragmatic politician he was. That is a fair and reasonable area to assess. All the Kennedys worked hard in their chosen field of politics and made the kind of compromises that any politician makes to be elected and re-elected. There always exists a gap between rhetoric and performance of any politician and it is up to us to judge if the size of that gap is acceptable.

The Kennedys did not lead as much as react to a world already changing. They were more pragmatic about the change than politicians who would militarily challenge the Soviet Union in knee-jerk fashion or rally around "segregation forever." Robert finally came to realize that proxy wars against communism on the Asian or any other continent could not be fought with willing recruits; young men no longer trusted their leaders. He also understood such wars were no substitute for a broader economic war that the Communists could not win. When he began to see that the political process he so believed in was failing many Americans, he chose to act. The politics of helping people attain a place in American society is neither liberal nor conservative. How people are helped creates ideological fractures. To him, "how" was not as important as acting—he was not an ideologue—as long as the job was done well he was satisfied.

The crowds that greeted Kennedy when he went to Delano, California on March 10, 1968 to show sympathy for Caesar Chavez and his farm workers' union grabbed at him so fiercely his hands were bleeding. During the ensuing campaign, this would often occur. His buttons, cuff links and tie clips would be snatched, they would grab at his hair. Later, during the campaign, every night after he greeted the crowds, Kennedy would have to nurse his bloody, swollen hands. "Well, so many people hate me that I have to give the people that love me a chance to get at me," said Bobby.

People either hated Bobby Kennedy or loved him. Many said they feared him. Once, when he was chief counsel for the Senate Select Committee on Improper Activities in the Labor of Management Fields (the McClellan committee), his questioning of a union official was so fierce, he made the Teamster cry. Yet there he was in the 1968 campaign, seeing a little girl with glasses in the crowd, blurting out: "You know something? My little girl has glasses just like yours. And I love my little girl very much," ending the short exchange with an affectionate squeeze at the back of the little girl's neck. The same man who would tenderly pick up poor, starving children whose skin was covered with open wounds, would unflinchingly stand toe-to-toe with Jimmy Hoffa even as the unspoken but nevertheless understood personal threat to Kennedy and his family hung in the air between them.

Much of Kennedy's contradictory reputation stemmed from the strict Roman Catholic beliefs of his mother, and the decidedly secular tone set by his father. He was easily the most devout of the nine children of Joseph and Rosemary Kennedy. One of the biggest ironies of the 1960 campaign for president is that John Kennedy, who was somewhat more skeptical than Robert about religion, had to face the issue of being a Roman Catholic. His sister Eunice once replied to the suggestion that a book be written about Jack's religious belief that the book would be a slim volume. Even if the Catholic issue was moot in Kennedy's 1968 campaign (McCarthy was a Catholic, too) someone said of the pair that McCarthy was "the bright professor who gave your bright son an A." Robert Kennedy "was the tough kid on the block who beat up your son on his way to school."[2]

Ethel Skakel was even more devout than her husband; she mainly attended Catholic schools (including Manhattanville College) and kept vessels of holy water in their home They said their rosaries frequently and regularly attended church. Robert questioned his children often about what they heard at the weekly service. When *Newsweek* ran a nude photo of Jane Fonda on its cover, Robert and Ethel were appalled. Divorce was so taboo to Ethel that when she encountered divorced friends at parties, she found it difficult to speak with them.

Did Kennedy's strong religious beliefs leave him with rigid principles of good and evil, as many claim? Certainly his religious beliefs, combined with shyness, made close relationships with his older, more worldly siblings, difficult for Bobby. He was the only one of the children to collect a $2,000 prize his father offered his children for abstaining from drinking or smoking until they reached twenty-one. His language had fewer of the profanities known to be in his brother Jack's colorful lexicon. For what he saw as venial sins, he was as forgiving and protective as only a good Catholic brother could be when faced with the president's now well-publicized sexual intrigues. He was less forgiving of the corrupt labor and businesses he methodically investigated in the 1950s. Their sins were purposeful, mortal ones.

If anyone could see the fabled "well-oiled Kennedy machine" on the day of his announcement, it had to be taken on faith. Kennedy boarded a commercial flight to New York City to march in the St. Patrick's Day Parade being held that day. Charter flights were de rigueur for serious presidential candidates. The "Kennedy magic" was tarnished a bit during that parade, his first appearance as an official presidential candidate. He drew mixed reviews from the onlookers. They included threats to beat him up, taunts from the largely Irish crowd calling him a traitor and one person ruing that Kennedy was protected by the police because he wanted to punch the senator in the mouth.

The anger from politicians and the press surprised even those who knew Kennedy would take a lot of heat for the manner in which he entered the race. It brought back all the old canards about the arrogant, unfeeling, overly ambitious Bobby Kennedy. Eugene McCarthy had braved the cold winter in New Hampshire—goes this line of thinking—to show that the Democratic Party's leader was beatable and perhaps a bad choice to face the Republican who it increasingly seemed would be Richard M. Nixon. Now that McCarthy had done the work, Kennedy was trying to run off with the prize. American liberals, in an advertisement in *The New York Times* were urged to choose between "rationality, courage and morality" and "irrationality, opportunism and amorality"; that is between McCarthy and Kennedy. McCarthy campaigners angrily criticized Robert Kennedy for not allowing them a few moments to savor their victory before crashing their party.

A few days later after Kennedy's announcement, as Schlesinger wrote, Jacqueline Kennedy spoke to him.

"Do you know what I think will happen to Bobby? The same thing that happened to Jack. . . . There is so much hatred in this country, and more people hate Bobby than hated Jack. . . . I've told Bobby this, but he isn't fatalistic, like me."

She was not the only person to voice such concerns. It was a regular topic of discussion among reporters covering the Kennedy campaign. And there were many enemies who hoped for such an outcome.

After the parade, Kennedy had a few meetings, made some phone calls, then took another commercial plane back to Washington. As his friend, journalist Jack Newfield, told the story, the airline terminal was oddly deserted. Only Kennedy and a few reporters were there. Kennedy's driver had not shown up and the latest candidate for president seemed tired. Robert Kennedy muttered sardonically as a possible suggestion for the reporters in the next day's papers: "The hero returns, and a huge throng turned out to greet him. It took the police to hold them back." He stood alone for a few moments until an airline employee came up to direct him to a waiting limousine. "How many in your party?" she inquired. "Just me, I'm alone," he replied.

Kennedy would rarely be so physically alone in the coming weeks. The crowds greeting Bobby often dangerously packed around him, nearly crushing him or themselves. Security men and advisors had to be quick to scoop up those who had fallen in front of the moving campaign car. The hazardous adulation for Bobby continued after his death. One child climbed a boxcar to watch Bobby's funeral train and accidentally touched a live wire. He lived, but people aboard the train could see his smoldering body.

Nineteen sixty eight was the most divisive year in America since the Civil War. People were battling in the streets and riots ripped open the inner cities of America; the stench of violence hung in the country's political air. Kennedy put himself into the heart of the battle willingly, as he had done since he took his first political job in 1953, working for Senator Joseph McCarthy. He did so with a kind of courage rare among politicians of any day. No one truly predicted his death, but it did not take a crystal ball to know that someone would make an attempt on his life.

Robert Kennedy put himself, finally, exactly, where he wanted to be when he announced his candidacy for president. He no longer had to satisfy his father, nor had a brother to protect. During nearly every part of his life he was in transition; Robert Kennedy lived in a constant state of becoming. Whatever the circumstances that brought him to the edge of himself, he took the last leap to get there on his own.

The what-ifs remain in the hearts and minds of those who remember him, who loved or despised him. Robert F. Kennedy participated thoroughly and inextricably in the action and passions of his times. He undeniably helped to define the politics of our age. That he remains part of our current political discourse is as high a praise as he would have wanted.

Bobby between LeMoyne Billings (l) and his roommate at Choate,
John F. Kennedy in Palm Beach, Florida, 1934.
(John F. Kennedy Library and Museum)

2

Enfant Terrible

> For, though I am not splenitive and rash,
> Yet I have something in me dangerous.
>
> *—Hamlet*

PROMPTNESS WAS A VIRTUE in the household where Bobby grew up. Lateness was not tolerated. The dinner call came as Robert, not quite five years old, was in the living room. He rushed through the passageway under the grand staircase that divided the living from the dining room. A separating door there slid on a groove and away into the wall. When Bobby rushed to the dinner table that time, the door was pulled fully out, not pushed into the wall. It was a glass door. He plunged ahead not seeing it. As his sister Pat tells the story, Bobby ran into the glass, smashed it and the pieces cut his head. There was blood all over. His mother Rose concluded that while her second son, Jack, was the worst at being prompt, Bobby was the most spectacular. He often plunged into life and the political stage. Robert was prone to the spectacular throughout his life. Among a family of overachievers, he strove to out-achieve them all.

When not yet four, Bobby jumped off a yawl and into Nantucket Sound to show that he "can too" swim. He could not swim, then. His brother Joe was there and pulled him out. "It showed," Jack Kennedy said about the incident, "either a lot of guts or no sense at all, depending on how you looked at it."

Many have looked at Robert Kennedy as reckless and believe his very public displays of fearlessness were a way to conquer inner demons. Those evil spirits were evidently pains that haunted him since childhood, torments of a youth who needed to show his siblings and parents that he, too, could be among them, compete with them. Critics say his torments, displayed as physical acts of recklessness, were really measures of his insecurity—disturbing enough to have disqualified him for public office.[1]

There is no doubt that Robert sought publicity for many of his physical exploits. But to twist that into a shallow psychoanalytic description of insecurity oversimplifies one of the most complex parts of Kennedy's personality. Such analysis ignores the fact that he had true physical courage. No other public person in the last fifty years was so marked by an ongoing threat to his life than Robert Kennedy, especially after the murder of his brother. Even before, with his unrelenting, very public crusade against crooked unions and racketeers, he lived each day with the notion that many of the men he investigated wanted him dead and had the means and inclination to carry out those wishes.

The presence of reporters and cameras does not lessen the fact that climbing mountains, entering coal mines, swimming among piranha and facing down rhinos is dangerous. Not many insecure people place themselves so obviously in harm's way. More likely the insecure hide behind bullet-proof glass, army's of body guards or just refuse to become involved in public life.

Robert alone among the Kennedy boys earned a varsity letter in college football, when by common measures he should not have been on the same football field as his teammates. The smallest, clumsiest, least likely athlete of the Kennedy boys became their most ardent sport participant. He dove into treacherous ocean waters, rode some of the worlds most dangerous rapids, made touch football the "official" Kennedy sport, played tennis and skied regularly. And when he competed or campaigned he disregarded the scrapes, cuts, chipped teeth and broken bones that resulted from rough competition—his own injuries or those suffered by others. Even when running for president, when day after day he had to soak his swollen, bloody hands that people mauled and scratched as they strained to touch him, it was a physical assault Kennedy took in stride. When he ran for president, he played down the ultimate injury many believed would come to him and that he expected.

Robert Kennedy was the shortest of the four brothers, a small, thin boy not as ruddy-cheeked as Ted nor as sickly as Jack. He came down with the normal range of childhood illnesses. He had his tonsils and adenoid removed, his teeth had to be straightened and he came down with pneumonia at age eleven. Yet he nearly always had to catch up to his brothers and sisters, try to compete with them. While they were all climbing trees like squirrels, said his sister Jean, Robert tended to fall out of the branches.[2]

Rose noted Robert's difficult position, seventh after two brothers and four sisters: "Our next child [after Robert] was our sweet and beautiful daughter Jean. And by the time Teddy arrived in 1932, Bobby was already more than seven years old. So there he was, with two older brothers [Jack being eight years older than Robert] and one very much younger, none of whom was much use to him as boyhood pals, playmates."[3] When Joseph Jr. and Jack got into boyhood brawls downstairs, Robert stayed upstairs with his sisters.

The Kennedy children were a raucous brood, always active, their lives heavily scheduled with sports, and raised to be sharply competitive. At one point, Rose decided to divide the family's porch with folding gates, two, three or four depending on the sit-

Street Fighting Man

There is no doubt Kennedy was an aggressive and tough competitor, whether it was in a senate hearing room or on a football field. He could be quick to anger especially when he believed a colleague or staff member was being lazy or untruthful. And there were several confrontations in his adult life that bordered on a fist fight.

Ronald Steel said in his book *In Love with Night* that if Kennedy had been born poor, he would have been a brawler and a drinker. This is a sly way of saying the man was a low-class bum. How the drunkenness applies is hard to fathom. Kennedy by all accounts was close to being a teetotaler. It may be a little Irish prejudice slipping into a poorly grounded assertion.

As often happens with Kennedy critics, to cinch an argument they will twist an incident to force a point. To argue Kennedy was a "street fighter" a street fight is helpful.

As Steel tells the story, it was Robert who got into a shouting match with some college students who were batting balls while playing touch football with Edward Kennedy and some friends. Steel said, without citing his source, it was brother Ted who pulls Bobby out of the argument before the game turns into a brawl.

The story is told differently in *No Final Victories* written by Lawrence O'Brien, who directed Jack's senate and presidential campaigns. O'Brien stood next to then-Senator Jack Kennedy, with crutches, on the sidelines watching the game.

It became apparent that the baseball players were hitting the balls into the Kennedy game and it was Ted who yelled for them to stop and who then exchanged angry words with them. A fight was about to start when Robert broke into the fray and said he would do the fighting, not his younger brother. "It was like a scene in ancient Rome, with both sides putting forth their gladiator," wrote O'Brien. Ted was bigger than his older brother, who was about thirty pounds lighter.

O'Brien suggested the senator might want to discreetly leave the scene in case police arrive. Jack refused to leave. The fight ends without a clear winner, but by O'Brien's estimation, with two badly banged up competitors. Later at dinner, Ethel notes her husband's bruised face, saying that it must have been some football game. "Yeah," was Robert's terse reply.

There is little disagreement that Bobby was more the football player than an intellectual. But in this instance, was he more the brawler or the brother protector? As Jack may have said, it all depends on how you look at it.

uation. "That way they could be with each other and entertain one another for hours at a time with minimal risk that they would push one another down or stick one another with something sharp or perhaps pile heavy objects inside or on top of the baby carriage." It was Robert in that baby carriage. This very protected child became the family's most ardent protector and daredevil.

Robert plunged into situations because that is what his siblings did, that is what his parents ingrained into all of their children. They believed in making their children secure—physically, economically, morally and above all with themselves and their family. One might see courage or recklessness in the way Kennedy plunged into things, but, as when he took the dive into the open waters at age four, he knew someone was around to pull him out. He was secure in knowing that he was not in real danger. When it was not his brothers, his wife, his family, his money, his social or political position that kept him from harm, Bobby's deep faith in himself and in God brought him security.

If insecurity played any part in Kennedy's life it came in the form of rootlessness: he lived in many homes and attended numerous schools (he did not remember exactly how many). Some of his teachers said too many. The first move came before Robert reached his first birthday in 1926; the already rich and legendary Joseph P. Kennedy Sr. found he had had enough of Boston. What he wanted for himself and his children could not be found among the city's so-called Brahmins. Like Boston's other, less prosperous Irish, he knew he no longer need apply.

The help wanted signs in businesses and well-to-do homes often appended the words "No Irish Need Apply." For the American-Irish generations that grew up after the nineteenth-century potato famine, particularly the Irish Catholic, these signs were superfluous. They knew they were unwanted by American

Protestants, Baptists and especially by the children of the American Revolution who dominated Boston's Brahmin society.

Joe Sr. strove to get more for his children than the snubs Boston society could give. That his daughters would not be invited to the galas of the debutantes nor his sons into the clubs of power weighed against Boston as the primary home of his growing family. He himself had been blackballed from a country club in Cohasset, Massachusetts.

"It was petty and cruel," Ralph Lowell, a Harvard University classmate of Joe Sr., recalled. Among the Brahmin elite, "who was Joe Kennedy but the son of Pat, the barkeeper?"[4]

The Lone Wolf of Wall Street had other concerns. His ambitions lay beyond the scions of New England. Boston was a backwater to someone making the kinds of fortunes available in the 1920s. Joe Sr. wanted to be closer to the action and far away from the poverty of the tormented Irish immigrants of his grandfathers' generation. He was already a prominent member of another, more important group than the Boston Brahmins: the world's capitalist club. So the Kennedys left Boston and its chilly reception behind; Joe Sr. was confident of even greater success closer to the bigger economic pond of New York City.

"I went to about twelve schools, at least," said Bobby, and then "shifted through a couple of private schools." He began school in Riverdale, New York's public system, then when the family moved to Bronxville and he was in third grade, attended Bronxville public schools. He also went to Gibbs School in London and attended St. Paul's prep (Concord, New Hampshire) Portsmouth Priory and, finally, Milton Academy, in Massachusetts.[5]

When he entered Milton Academy, someone told Joe Sr. his son's poor scholastic performance was directly due to his academic rootlessness. His grades were bad enough for his housemaker, Albert Norris, to write Robert's parents that he was close to being held back a year. Joe Sr. made the trip up to Milton to discuss the situation with Norris.

"He no sooner gets in a school situation than he is pulled out, put into a new school situation, with different methods of teaching, different rules and regulations," Norris told the globe-trotting father. "He has no roots. He is always on the move. It's no wonder his grades are so low."[6]

"He was a very intelligent boy, quiet and shy, but not outstanding, and he left no special mark on Milton," noted Emily Perry, widow of headmaster Arthur B. Perry at Milton Academy.[7] Thomas G. Cleveland, who later was head of the religious department, and knew Bob when he was a student there himself, declared, "He came and he went."

Kennedy finally was able to enter Harvard University. Yet even then he was no scholar, content to concentrate more on his physical education than a scholarly course. When it came time to choose a law school, his undergraduate performance was meager according to the standards of Harvard Law School, which would not allow his entry. Robert settled for University of Virginia Law School. He performed better there, but did not shine academically. Yet he was the first son to earn a law degree and to acquire a profession, although he never truly intended to practice law and never did. As his brothers before him, Robert's direction would steer toward a career in public service.

Robert had Joe Sr.'s pale blue eyes, many have noted, and he taught his third son to be tenacious in his pursuit of his goals, not to think twice about using power if necessary. It was Joe Sr. who often drove business competitors into bankruptcy without pity or regret and Robert who bruised egos during his first thirty-five years.[8] So which was it with Robert Kennedy? Quiet and shy or tough and ego bruising? Both.

That Kennedy could seem so much of one thing and another, that he could appear Janus-faced is because he had two separate standards to follow: the tough, secular-minded father and the more spiritual mother who instilled notions of duty to God, his neighbors and himself. Both mother and father stressed discipline, although the mother was more present during Robert's early years. Some believe it was Robert's piety that accounted for his early rigid personality: his "black and white" thinking that saw the world simply divided into good and evil. His siblings found his prudishness off-putting; coming home to Hyannis Port, Robert found Jack, back from Harvard, in the living room with several friends, talking and laughing. "Aren't you glad to see me?" Bobby asked after no one noticed or greeted him.[9]

Bobby's brand of Catholicism tended toward a more inclusive and forgiving tone than a fire and brimstone, "woe to the sinners" variety. He publicly challenged a Catholic priest who preached that all non-Catholics would be damned. And while he may not have liked his sister's marriage outside the Church, he did name his first daughter after Kathleen. No brother was as loyal as Bobby despite Jack's womanizing, which must have been an anathema to the pious younger brother. Yet he stuck by Jack time and time again. Only when it came time for Robert Kennedy to take the role of power wielder, the secular politician, the tough prosecutor, campaign manager, cabinet officer—some of the many roles that his father sought for his sons—did the brash, rigid, hard young man emerge.

The softer Bobby, the one who sought racial equality, justice for the disenfranchised and help for the poor came from his religious training and beliefs. He lived with a loving and forgiving God. His enemies were secular ones; he did not affix them with a scarlet letter E for evil. Joe Sr. liked his third son's "direct" manner and Arthur Krock of *The New York Times*, noted the son had the same capacity for likes and dislikes, love and hate as his father. Exactly. It was not a puritan zeal that drove Bobby, the brash young man; it was an outsider's polemic, the kind instilled by an Irish Catholic father desiring to break into the Protestant social world: the barkeeper's son demanding, an equal place among the Boston Brahmins. And if Joe Sr. could not win them over, even as ambassador to the Court of St. James, the ruthless, tough-minded capitalist was going to make damn sure that his sons could.

Bobby began to feel sick and there was nothing he could do until the plane could land in Omah in Eastern Soviet Union. During the flight, Kennedy shook all over and felt freezing cold, except for his head, which was very hot, wrote the senate counsel in his diary. His temperature was nearing 100°F. William O. Douglas, the Supreme Court Justice, who was Bobby's traveling companion, decided to call for a doctor. They were deep inside the Soviet Union, and the dogmatic Cold Warrior Kennedy balked: "No Communist is going to doctor me." It got worse. Three hours later the "Communist doctor" showed up and the doctor was a woman.

By the time she arrived Kennedy's fever was over 100°F and he was quite possibly experiencing delirium. The local doctor probably suffered from an ardent anti-Communist harangue of a sick, rich young man used to the world's best medical care. "She evidently didn't have her penicillin with her, and so used mine. Had a hell of a time finding my pulse and sticking the needle into me," Kennedy wrote in his diary of the 1955 trip to Soviet Central Asia. The Communist doctor stayed with him all day, and the next two. It was not until he arrived in Moscow several days later that Robert remembered to thank the doctor "for coming out at night."[10] Gratitude in the defense of liberty evidently was a vice.

It was one of Kennedy's least likeable traits that he was a "rather dead than Red" anti-Communist. Throughout the

Robert F. Kennedy taking the plunge.
(John F. Kennedy Library and Museum)

diaries of his travels in the 1950s are sprinkled superfluous challenges to "commies." It got so bad on the 1955 trip that Douglas
had to berate Kennedy: "You can never argue with these fellows
so why don't we just forget about it, and spend the evening doing
something rather than wasting it trying to convert some guy
who will never be converted?" Douglas finally got Robert to
relent, but the knee-jerk Red-baiter temperament took years of
experience to cool.

Throughout the 1950s and into the presidency of his brother,
Kennedy acted as if he were a boy scout trying to earn a merit badge
in the Cold War. It was this trait that led him to take another
plunge: into the gnarly world of Joseph R. McCarthy and the hunt
for Communist infiltrators. He became assistant counsel to the
Senate Permanent Subcommittee on Investigations in early 1953.

Jack advised against it. He did not like McCarthy's tactics and
thought it would hurt his brother's career in the long run. Robert
was adamant, although he later regretted his decision. "I thought
there was a serious internal security threat to the United States; I
felt at the time that Joe McCarthy seemed to be the only one who
was doing anything about it," Bobby said much later. "I was wrong."

Joe Sr. had few misgivings about his son's joining the
McCarthy committee. It was Bobby's father who asked
McCarthy to hire his son, but the Kennedys wanted Robert to
be the chief counsel. That infamous role went instead to Roy
Cohn. It was the committee's tactics under Cohn, and an evident
dislike the two young attorneys had of each other, that eventually led to Kennedy resigning his position. Robert Lovett, an
investment banker who had met Robert during the McCarthy
hearings, was introduced to Joe Sr. "That's pretty tough company he's traveling with," Lovett told Joe Sr., meaning particularly
Cohn, "who seemed about as unpleasant a character as one
could find in a day's march." Joe Sr. said, "Well, put your mind

at rest about that. Bobby is just as tough as a bootheel."[11]

Tough as Robert Kennedy might have been, he irrevocably stained his image with liberals. Adam Yarmolinsky, professor of law, noted that Kennedy's association with McCarthy had to be clarified, and could be satisfactorily explained, "but anything that has to be explained is going to present a problem because the explanation never catches up with the charge."[12]

Kennedy had little to do with the Communist-seeking part of the McCarthy committee. Instead, he was assigned to look into the sales of war matériel and other goods shipped to China by American allies during the Korean War. Except for those cited for trading with the Chinese, who were the primary backers of the North Koreans, most reports praised Kennedy for his work; few challenged his facts. There was some legitimate complaints that the investigator's conclusions were a naïve misunderstanding about the role of world trade, that many of the ships were there to carry away goods, not deliver them. There is little doubt that Kennedy and his staff assembled an impressive amount of facts, digging into a vast amount of shipping records to cull a scandalous record of trade with Western Europe and China. The attention he received paled compared to his rival Roy Cohn.

Maybe it was a good thing that Bobby had what amounted to a practice run. While Kennedy prepared himself well to present his findings, his presentation of self may not have sparked confidence among observers. LaVern Duffy, an investigator for the committee, noted Bobby's appearance: shirt open, necktie pulled down and shirt sleeves rolled up past the elbows. Bobby also wore white, athletic socks with his suit. And Duffy noted Bobby's demeanor in May 1953 when he made his first public presentation as assistant counsel—a general nervousness and his hands trembling while his wife and sister looked on.[13] Kennedy never became a great orator, but over the years he trained himself to become a passable one. Not so in May 1953. It was Bob Kennedy's presentation of fact that won him praise.

Kennedy came through the experience mostly unbruised. He had a mostly unassailable "motherhood issue" to investigate. Any shipments to an enemy at time of war was difficult, if not impossible to explain away to the public while "our boys are dying at the front." The Republicans did not try. When McCarthy was persuaded by fellow Senator Stuart Symington (D-Missouri) to send a letter to President Eisenhower asking what the official policy was regarding wartime shipments and our allies, McCarthy agreed. However, Vice President Richard M. Nixon saw a Democratic trap, and convinced McCarthy the letter was a subtle ruse intended to embarrass the Republican administration. McCarthy ordered the letter, which had already been delivered, to be retrieved. It was.

Two months after delivering his report, Robert Kennedy resigned his position as counsel to the majority. Six months later, he would rejoin as counsel for the minority, opposed to McCarthy. Then the sparks flew, including a near-physical confrontation with Roy Cohn. But Robert's first plunge into national politics left him less than enthused. All his hard work garnered small attention compared to the main show, which was as much based on gaining publicity as it was on ensuring America's national security. Wrote Kennedy:

With two exceptions, no real research was ever done. Most of the investigations were instituted on the basis of some preconceived notion by the chief counsel or his staff members and not on the basis of any information that had been developed. Cohn and Schine claimed they knew from the outset what was wrong; and they were not going to allow the facts to interfere. Therefore no real spade work was ever undertaken. I thought

Senator McCarthy made a mistake in allowing the committee to operate in such a fashion, told him so and resigned.[14]

Kennedy once again took a plunge into dangerous waters and found them uninviting. What kept him out of danger this time was his own hard work and refusal to join what he saw as a destructive course. Joining the McCarthy committee turned out not to be a reckless endeavor, but it forever tainted him with people who saw McCarthy's tactics as dangerous and demagogic. Kennedy made a mistake and later admitted it. When he rejoined the committee he became a member of the opposition to McCarthy, a "loyal opposition" since he remained personally loyal to the censured senator: defending him at times in loud, public arguments with friends, visiting the senator when he was sick and near death, then attending McCarthy's funeral. The young Cold Warrior had years of explaining ahead of him.

Robert Kennedy was at an interlude in his life. Instead of taking up what his resignation letter said he would, private law practice, he joined his father as his staff assistant on the Commission on Reorganization of the Executive Branch. It was run by ex-President Herbert Hoover. This was the time Kennedy became involved in a brawl while playing touch football in a Georgetown park. He "met" his biographer Arthur M. Schlesinger Jr. during this time, through a squabble in the letters columns of *The New York Times* (Kennedy had a conservative opinion about the 1945 Yalta Conference agreement, condemning it). Jack, as usual, was able to better handle the situation: "My sisters are mad at you because of the letter you wrote about Bobby," he told Schlesinger.

The same month Robert left the McCarthy committee, its Democratic members began a boycott, walking out in order to protest the sole control McCarthy had over the hiring and firing of committee staff. When the Republicans relented in January 1954, the minority members were given a chance to appoint a counsel of their own. Kennedy was given the job. An abortive start to his public career would turn into a national spotlight for Bobby. He used the new position to show contempt for what he thought was a time-wasting hunt for Communist subversion. Then, when midterm elections changed the balance of power in the senate, he turned the committee's attention to what became one of the central themes of his life: the fight against organized crime.

There's one more thing about the impetuous boy and the man who some thought dove recklessly into danger. Bobby was a man of passions, but was rarely impulsive on important matters. He held a pool of aggression that often displayed itself physically, at times violently. The emotions showed through; many saw his impatience with cocktail party chit chat, the boredom with the details of governing and his inability to keep that campaign smile permanently affixed.

While he often displayed a physical bravado for television cameras and reporters, if one looks carefully at each mountain climbed, rhino challenged or river rapid paddled, none of it overestimated his own capacity. Robert early on made himself into a strong and self-assured athlete. Each and every physical challenge displayed an accurate knowledge of his limits. Had he overstepped his limits, Kennedy could have truly had a dangerous presence. What looks like a reckless streak to the rest of us mounted on comfortable cushions and chairs in front of the television was more like a performance by a highly trained professional.

What could make him dangerous, what sometimes did push him too far, was a reckless disregard for procedure and established constitutional practice.

Senate candidate Robert F. Kennedy.
(© *The New York Times* (Burns))

3

A Splendid Ruthlessness

The easiest way to get a reputation is to go outside the fold,
shout around for a few years . . . and then crawl back to the shelter.
—*F. Scott Fitzgerald*

TWO DECISIONS MASSACHUSETTS GOVERNOR Paul Dever made in the spring of 1952 changed the course of Robert Kennedy's career and labeled him for life. First, Dever decided he would run for reelection. This was crucial because that same year, when the country would be choosing a new president, Massachusetts had a United States Senator to elect. Republican Henry Cabot Lodge Jr., the third-term incumbent, was a powerful presence in the state. Governor Dever nearly alone among Democrats could challenge Lodge, who looked to be unbeatable. Only one Massachusetts politician beyond Dever had the audaciousness and money to challenge the incumbent senator: John F. Kennedy.

Dever had considered running for senator and whether Jack Kennedy would oppose him was in question. Jack was mindful of the divisive effect a primary challenge would have on the Democratic changes in the fall and his own career. He did not want to continue in the congress, however. The Kennedys had done private polling; they thought the old-time politician Dever could lose to the young war hero. Speculation ended on April 6, Palm Sunday, when Dever told Jack he would run for a third gubernatorial term. The two were not close politically or personally; Dever was from Joseph P. Kennedy Sr.'s generation and Joe Sr. was out of touch with the state's politics by as much as twenty years. Jack showed he knew Massachusetts politics better than anyone.

In the beginning, the two candidates decided to run separate campaigns, except for a few districts in and close to Boston. Jack wanted to emphasize youth and that he was not tied to the Boston political machine. Dever probably thought he could be hurt by the inexperienced young man's campaign organization. The older politician was right, at first.

By the end of May, the charismatic congressman was campaigning hard around the state and heading for complete disaster. As Kenneth P. O'Donnell, who was working for the campaign, put it, the "well-oiled" Kennedy organization was so disorganized it had failed to get off the ground. O'Donnell said he had been waiting for three months for a statewide organization to get started, and by that point, none existed or was imminent. "Here it is the end of May, and we haven't appointed a single Kennedy chairman or organizer in any city in Massachusetts," O'Donnell told Jack.[1] Even Jack's father could not successfully fund a campaign to buy an election if no campaign organization existed.

Meanwhile in an old courthouse near the Brooklyn Bridge a twenty-six-year-old assistant attorney in the Justice Department had some concerns of his own. He had been on the job since December and did not have an office or even a desk. Robert Kennedy worked in the library or any open desk he could find. The other assistant attorneys had two-room offices. The "millionaire's son" was making $4,000 a year (which was about $800 more than the rest of the assistant attorney general staff). Nobody paid much attention to him. Robert was an obscure member of an unheralded division of the Justice Department. Nor did he earn his position as a political appointment on his own. Joe Kennedy Sr. arm-twisted Senator Joseph R. McCarthy, whose committee staff Bobby would later join, into getting his son the job.[2]

Kennedy worked that first job as a nobody, earning what was for him a pittance, without recognition from his fellow workers or even his own brother the congressman. And one could not have pried the young man away from his job for love or money. The work he did was his own, doing something away from under the shadows of his father and brother. His ambitions were as fiercely felt as the rest of the Kennedys'. Nobody could get him away. "Don't drag me into it," Bobby told O'Donnell when the latter called him. He loved what he was doing at the Justice Department and knew nothing of Massachusetts politics. Kennedy feared he would make the situation worse.[3] After two more phone calls from O'Donnell, Bobby agreed to talk to his father.

Not love or money, but Joe Sr. had enough paternal influence on his third son to convince him to quit what was becoming an interesting assignment, to join what looked to be by most observers a losing cause, involving himself in a world he little knew nor liked: Massachusetts politics.

O'Donnell said he did not know what Joe Sr. told Robert. He remembers only that while playing golf a few days later, a call came from his Harvard University football buddy: "I am with Jack and my mother and my sisters at a big tea party with a couple of thousand women in Quincy [Massachusetts], thanks to you. I hope you're satisfied. Get down here right away. I want you to tell Jack some of that stuff you've been telling me."[4] Jack had plenty of old and new political hands working for him who knew Massachusetts and could assist him in forming political strategy. What he needed was someone who could manage a campaign's details while being able to handle the formidable presence of his father. He found both in his younger brother.

The second decision Governor Dever made that changed Robert Kennedy's life came after the September primary, where Jack picked up far more votes for his senate bid than Dever did for reelection. Both unopposed, Kennedy got seventy-five percent of the votes while Dever got sixty percent. After that, Dever's campaign organization tried to move into Kennedy campaign headquarters in several cities. He now wanted a Kennedy-Dever campaign. The Kennedys, Jack and Robert that is, wanted to stay with the original idea. Joe Sr. told them to let Dever work with them. They argued with their father. Jack told Robert: "Don't give into them, but don't get involved in it. Treat it as an organizational problem." Robert followed his brother's instructions closely, but without the tact that Jack may himself have employed.

Bobby himself described his meeting with Dever as a "debacle" and said Dever became furious with him.[5] But the strategy worked. Dever was mad at Robert, not Jack. Joe Sr. smoothed over the relationship between the two campaigns ("Keep that fresh kid of yours out of sight," Dever told Joe Sr.). Electing his brother was Kennedy's prime concern: "What the people were saying about me was rather unimportant."

Old-time politicking did not impress the young campaign manager, either. As O'Donnell tells the story, some of Boston's older politicians would hang around Kennedy's political headquarters reminiscing. One member of the group, who once campaigned for mayor by singing "Danny Boy" from a sound truck, became annoyed when no one in the office, including Bobby, recognized him. "You call this a political headquarters?" Bobby threw him out.

Robert Kennedy offended the old pols of Boston, was rude and unsympathetic to them. John and Robert had little time to schmooze; all their energies had to focus on beating Lodge and the old-time politicians were no longer relevant to how modern campaigns would be won. Robert and his brother were pioneering a new kind of campaigning—one that began to see the value of "packaging" a candidate. Jack worked harder presenting himself directly to potential voters than to politicos. His father took care of the pols. Jack's 1952 senate campaign was a bridge between the old and new type of politician. The crusty veterans who spent their political lives choosing the candidates were beginning to lose control; they knew it and they resented it. Especially national politics started relying more on the image of a candidate rather than their relationship with power brokers. National interest groups were becoming more powerful, too, as the expense of political campaigns started to grow.

Paul Dever was part of the last hurrah of Boston pre-war politics. Like the changes the Civil War brought to the American scene, so World War II changed everything. America was unquestionably the leading power; nearly every other pre-war power had been devastated. The Civil War capitalists began the "gilded age" as the money and power won in World War II began years of prosperity in the United States. Two differences between the post-Civil War and World War II changed the kind of people who went to Washington in the twentieth century. Nineteenth-century young men had a vast amount of new land to settle. Pioneering new businesses and development of the West took up their energies. America busied itself with consolidation and growth. Its new wealth, military strength and oceans buffering each end of the country kept it relatively safe from foreign intervention.

Washington, D.C. itself in that era could not attract the country's best potential leaders. Unlike the capitals of Europe, London or Paris say, which were social and business centers, Washington could only claim itself the seat of government. Few wanted to abandon their families and circle of friends, their professions and local public duties to serve in the then swampy national capital. That changed in the twentieth century. Especially after the Roosevelt administration enlarged the scope of the federal government and World War II shifted the balance of power toward it. Washington, D.C. became a more interesting and challenging place to serve. Men who might have preferred seeking power and interesting careers in business now had management of a world power, the world's leading power, to consider for a career. Men like the Kennedys could find greater satisfaction leading the country during the Cold War than any business could provide. Washington, D.C. left its backwater origins behind in the 1940s.

Neither Jack nor Robert Kennedy had much affinity for Boston or local politics. Part of that had to do with the nature of Jack Kennedy's interest: "I had no background particularly [in politics], in my family we were interested not so much in the ideas of politics as in the mechanics of the whole process."[6] Robert Kennedy followed his brother's footsteps and became as interested as he in the "gamesmanship" of politics. Jack Kennedy also had more interest in foreign affairs and the intrigues of the Cold War. With Robert again following his brother's lead, the Kennedys must have been impatient with the methods politicians from their father's and grandfathers' generations employed. Neither came into politics with a political philosophy or moral commitment and had little regard for "the gregarious, often transparent, mannerisms and crude, patronage-based approach of machine pols."[7] The main difference between Jack and Bobby was temperament. Jack could cover his emotions; Bobby, the more passionate of the two, could not.

Politicians who spent careers in doling out services to their constituents in the wards and precincts of America's cities were finding their people moving out of cities they controlled. National highways and television began to connect a nation like no rail-road or canal ever could. The Kennedys were young, smart and had unlimited amounts of energy (and money) and they knew it. Dever and his generation resented that, resented the end of their brand of politics and most of all resented being pushed around by a tough, very young campaign manager who did not know them nor care about what they had done for Boston.

Bobby's mean reputation began from such "last hurrah" encounters. Young, aggressive and unconcerned about anything but electing his brother, Kennedy knew the effect his attitude would have on Boston's political clique. It did not matter. Nothing mattered except electing his brother senator.

Jack not only found someone who could manage his campaign and his father, he also found a foil. In subsequent campaigns and during his presidency, Jack often used his brother to tell people "no" without damaging his own reputation. The effect on Robert's image was the opposite. With each subsequent incident, Bobby's notoriety for ruthlessness grew. It would interfere significantly much later, when Bobby ran for president. Nearly anything Robert did from 1952 on was measured by a ruthlessness quotient singular to him. Kennedy detractors cite ruthlessness so often and so unremittingly it often seems as if Robert were the only politician who made pragmatic, tough decisions. Bobby gets bashed in terms Faustian or Machiavellian, the ultimate dark princes.

The trouble with that argument is the miscues and tactlessness, the debacles, probably had simpler, less grand causes. The young lawyer was inarticulate, unworldly and as yet unequipped to ease his way through the thickets of political relationships with skill and grace. It can be argued that he never mastered these finer arts of politics. Bobby's fierce competitive spirit easily made him enemies. The young Kennedy was clumsy among strangers even in private encounters and ungainly in larger social events. An unseen ugly duckling boy still existed inside the highly visible campaign manager who by all accounts was well-liked by his staff and could inspire them like a varsity football coach. Each campaign day Bobby would lead by his personal work ethic. Even people who served as his loyal opposition over the years credit him with a doggedness and penchant for working long hours. Bobby's poor social skills needed more attention.

"My brother Jack couldn't be here," Kennedy told a crowd when he was forced into giving a speech during the 1952 campaign. "My sister Eunice couldn't be here. My mother couldn't be here. My sister Jean couldn't be here. But if my brother Jack were here, he'd tell you that Lodge has a very bad voting record. Thank you." This hardly demonstrates the sharp tongue of a ruthless manipulator.

He had "that little stammer,"[8] one campaign worker remembered, and a brusque manner. She noted, "Bobby was very abrasive, as he always was with *certain* [italics added] people. And yet he hopped right into it, the way he did with everything. He was in his shirt sleeves all the time. He'd do anything. He'd lug cartons and seal envelopes." David Powers, a close Kennedy aide, remembered a bridge running from North Station to Charlestown that the local campaign manager had trouble placing an "ELECT JOHN F. KENNEDY FOR SENATOR" sign there. A ladder barely reached it and Bobby climbed it to the top rung; "the only people I saw that high up were firemen."

Robert Kennedy was physically fearless and socially awkward. The ruthless reputation confused those who knew him in a different way than the old Boston pols did. His friends described a sensitive, shy boy and young man. Those with whom he competed knew a different, tougher man. When people met him in person, they could hardly believe the notorious hand they shook belonged to Bobby.

The Soles of Robert Kennedy

Robert Kennedy could rub people the wrong way. No doubt about that. Thomas A. Parrott could tell you. He worked for Maxwell D. Taylor, who became an important member of the Kennedy administration. At one point, Taylor was selected to be chairman of the Special Group for Counterinsurgency (CI). Parrott was CI's secretary and was blunt about one member of the group: "Bobby, in my view, was an unprincipled sinister little bastard."

CI's secretary was upset that the attorney general arrived late to the meetings, then put his feet on the table, "so others had to look at the soles of his shoes." Kennedy wanted Arthur Goldberg, secretary of labor and later named to the Supreme Court by President Kennedy, to join the group. Goldberg attended a previous meeting and Taylor and Parrott thought, according to the latter, he talked too much. Taylor told Kennedy no. Kennedy said "in effect," he would have to talk to his brother. Each member of the committee backed down, but Taylor. "Well, we're not going to have him." Final.

"Whereupon Bobby pushed his notebook closed, said, 'Oh shit, the second most powerful man in the country loses another one,' and flounced out of the room, like a child, slamming the door."[9]

Another version of the incident adds information the above version left out: Taylor and Kennedy became close personal friends when the two worked together on a post-mortem of the Bay of Pigs invasion. Ethel Kennedy said her husband "worshiped" Taylor and considered him a "renaissance man." The Kennedys named one of their sons after Taylor.

This account says the incident was "amusing" and that Bobby became belligerent and threatening, so everyone at the table folded but Taylor. "No, Bobby, it would not be right to add him to the group." This account has Robert saying, "Shit, the second most important man . . ." etc, then pushing back his chair, banging down his briefing book before stalking out of the room, slamming the door.[10]

A third version[11] notes Taylor had an aversion to large committees. While "Bobby successfully pressed the others to vote for Goldberg's participation," Taylor "cheerfully ignored the vote." Here, Kennedy "snapped" the key phrase, "Well, shit," and etc., slamming the door. Taylor wanted to leave no doubt among the members who was in charge of the committee even if "Taylor sometimes had to remind [Kennedy] of who was chairman."[12]

Whether Kennedy stalked or flounced out of the room is of little consequence. But that Taylor and Kennedy had a close working and personal relationship is key to understanding the exchange. At worst being turned down was a minor irritation to a powerful, busy man used to getting his way. It sounds more like someone, half in jest, submitting to a much older (Taylor was in his sixties) and respected man.

Soon, Kennedy would contribute to his ruthless reputation on his own, without the help of his brother or family, as he entered the world of corrupt unions, organized crime and faced Jimmy Hoffa.

A strange man entered the offices of Robert Kennedy, who was by then, 1955, serving as chief counsel to the Senate Permanent Subcommittee on Investigations. Had Kennedy been working as a movie executive, office workers would have simply assumed central casting sent the man. The stranger's long black curls ran down the back of his neck and he was dressed in a black coat, black pants and a black shirt. He could have easily been mistaken for a character actor in the role of a gangster. The stranger was a gangster: Joey Gallo. He would be appearing before the committee to testify about organized crime's influence on the corruption of labor unions.

Gallo felt the office rug when he walked in, saying it would be a nice place for a crap game. When another visitor arrived, Gallo promptly frisked him. "No one is going to see Mr. Kennedy with a gun on him. If Kennedy gets killed now everybody will say I did it. And I am not going to take the rap." A secretary in the office could have determined her own salary by taking a job offered by Gallo, who said the money would come from her taking as much as she wanted from the till.[13]

It is easy to paint the character of gangsters as Runyonesque, colorful, small-time operators who only involve themselves in providing the "victimless" services such as gambling (legal gambling was just underway in Las Vegas). The truth is that they were, and are, hoodlums whose reach is vast and who, up until the early 1960s, were virtually untouched by federal officials who were more concerned about the threat of communism. Like his investigation of trade with China during the Korean War,

Robert Kennedy found an issue he believed could not have political negatives.

Gallo once appeared before a judge, as a suspect in a case where the murdered man was shot so many times in the face he was unrecognizable. Particularly compelling testimony by a victim of Gallo's gangster brand of terrorist tactics gave the committee a glimpse into Gallo's methods, this time involving the distribution of jukeboxes.

> He [a Gallo henchman] kept pounding away at my head and face and it got to a point where I was just barely able to keep my head up. Every time I started to plead, Panarella would lift a napkin holder, [the kind] used in luncheonettes, with the open face on both sides about ten inches high—he lifted it in his hand and said he would bash my skull in if I said anything else.[14]

When the Democrats took control of the senate in 1955, Kennedy was named chief counsel to the Senate Committee on Investigations. Robert despised the years Joseph R. McCarthy squandered with his hunt for Communists in the American government, believed their threat nearly nil. He sought another area of inquiry that would satisfy his ambition and justify the committee's time. Union officials who stole money from their members, gangsters who mostly aided by wresting control of "honest" unions and enforcing the authority of the union bosses, could garner attention for an ambitious, young man who wanted to make public service, politics, his career. And it could get him a lot of attention—fast.

Kennedy dealt with his "witnesses" in a harsh and unrelenting manner that was criticized at the time. Teamster president David Beck, one of the chief subjects of the investigation, described Robert as overeager, intolerant, vicious; some observers compared Bobby's questioning to the tactics of Joseph

Robert and Jack at the rackets committee hearings.
(© UPI)

Robert campaigns for Jack in the 1960 primary for president.
(© *Look* (Lerner))

The Kennedy sons with father Joseph P. Kennedy:
(l to r) Joseph Jr., John and Robert.
(John F. Kennedy Library and Museum)

McCarthy. During the hearings, Robert revealed a side that saw the confrontation simply as between good and evil, "white hats against black hats." "You haven't got the guts to [answer], have you?" Kennedy asked Joey Glimco, president of the Chicago branch of the Teamsters. It seemed as much a personal battle as a legislative discovery of facts. Kennedy went as far, in his book on the investigations, *The Enemy Within*, to paint these rough men with an effeminate brush: riding up the elevator to his office he smells a heavy odor of perfume and wonders what "madam" would be testifying that day. "Walking down the hall with Glimco to the caucus room, [I] realized that he was the source of the oppressive odor." Not only were his enemies cowardly crooks, they smelled bad too.

The young investigator's seeming disregard of legal process added to Kennedy's ruthless reputation. He needed to "prove" he was right (a legislative committee's function is to gather information) as if he were a prosecuting attorney. Much of the testimony seemed designed to put his "witnesses" behind bars. Even the sympathetic and exhaustive biographer of Robert Kennedy Arthur M. Schlesinger Jr. had to admit that some critics, in this case Professor Alexander Bickel of Yale Law School writing in *The New Republic*, had "a genuinely forceful apprehension—that Kennedy in these matters had displayed an excess of zeal, that he was a man driven by a conviction of righteousness, a fanaticism of virtue, a certitude about guilt that vaulted over gaps in evidence." Bickel wrote: "Mr. Kennedy knows, and when he knows he is very sure that he knows." Bickel characterized Kennedy as one who sees public service as a matter of ends and not means.

Not everyone saw it that way. After an afternoon of testimony by David Beck, Kennedy closed out the session with his own questioning of the Teamster president, pushing the corrupt union head into taking the Fifth Amendment sixty-five times. *Chicago*

Daily News reporter Edwin A. Lahey said the closing half hour of the session "was about the finest job I've ever seen done on Capitol Hill. If ever a Providential justice was ladled out in the Caucus room, you did it that day."

Robert Kennedy understood from firsthand observation how well a senate committee can operate to bring publicity to a cause and to the promoter of the cause. He was more thorough than Joseph McCarthy. Kennedy and his staff worked hard and genuinely strove to ferret out real cases of corruption and criminal activity while McCarthy settled for hearsay and innuendo. Had Kennedy been genuinely ruthless about the use of his committee, he could have chosen an easier way to feed his ambition.

Kennedy knew he was making a name for himself and in a very public manner. Despite warnings from both his brother Jack and his father, that it would hurt Jack's reelection chances for the senate in 1958, and maybe the presidency later on, while alienating the unions, Robert Kennedy plunged ahead. He shrewdly understood the politics of the situation better than both those family advisors. By the end of the hearings in 1959, Robert Kennedy probably was more well-known than his brother Jack. Once, when Jack was on a plane on a trip from Boston to Washington, a woman sitting next to him said, "Aren't you afraid that those terrible labor union racketeers will do something to your seven lovely children?" Jack said, "That's not me. That's my brother." Just before they left the plane, the woman said to him, "I hope your brother gets to be president." "That's not my brother, that's me," Jack replied. The story might be apocryphal, but its charm was based on Robert's newly-won fame.

Senator Kennedy continued to advise his brother against the investigation, even as the special committee was voted a budget and staff. He finally acquiesced and joined the committee himself (archconservative Senator Strom Thurmond of South

Carolina would have gotten the position if Jack did not accept). Jack could hardly refuse Robert's request that he needed him; Robert had helped Jack in his senate campaign even though he wanted to remain in his first job as an attorney for the Justice Department in 1952. His father was bitterly opposed and was furious with his son. Robert was determined despite all this. Joe Sr. and Jack were wrong. It put their son and brother in the spotlight like no other issue could have. And although both Kennedys became identified in the minds of the public with the hearings, it was Bobby's investigation all the way.

As Jimmy Hoffa put it, in his own inimitable style before the Beck testimony: "It was like shooting rats in a barrel." In a single, succinct phrase the man who would replace Beck as Teamster president and be Bobby's antonymic doppelgänger for years to come, caught the contradictions of the situation perfectly. The people he was investigating with such zeal *were* gangsters, rats. They were vicious crooks and murderers who stole from businesses and unions alike. Unlike the romantic movie images, these gangsters had no qualms about threatening the people who stood in their way, their family members and friends. Businessmen, union members and journalists were beaten, murdered; in one case blinded with acid, by the people Robert Kennedy brought in front of the senate committee. It took a "ruthless" investigator to open this underworld to the full attention of the public. That excess in the investigation of racketeers and crooked labor unions was possible did not enter Bobby's mind when he put the hearings in motion.

Furthermore, it was not like Kennedy to choose an enemy that was helpless (as McCarthy and his legislative counsel Roy Cohn had done). Many of the crooked labor officials had extensive political backing to protect themselves. These people were fully capable of vengeance; retribution was their way of life.

Kennedy himself became the target of many threats both to him and his family. He believed his brother's murder could have been the result of a conspiracy by gangsters that he himself had flushed out from their dark holes of corruption.

Many critics have said that Bobby *acted* tough. The "little brother" needed to conceal his vulnerability to compete with his older brothers. Maybe. It is not contradictory, however, to say that while he may have acted tough, he was tough. Easier targets were available to propel the young, aggressive investigator. Politicians pick welfare mothers and small-time drug users and other such targets for a reason: they have little in the way to defend themselves. Few politicians had Bobby's daring. He actively and with all his energy sought out enemies as dangerous as exist anywhere. Had Robert Kennedy been truly ruthless, he would not have been so willing to be the enemy of such infamous people.

The characterization of Kennedy as ruthless would come up time and time again. Its next incarnation would come when he resigned from the McClellan committee to manage the campaign of his brother for president. Jack's 1960 campaign probably cemented Robert's image. Now it was not just the brash young man, but the tough, prosecutorial senate counsel who was entering the campaign and few Democrats cheered the prospect.

Why anyone would need to visit Disneyland when the typical national campaign for president is as wild a roller-coaster ride as one can have in this life remains a mystery, but there they were. The 1960 campaign for president was in full swing and many of Jack Kennedy's campaign aides had decided to take an afternoon off to visit Disneyland while the campaign was in Los Angeles. "Some of you think Disneyland is more important than nominating the next president of the United States. Those that do can resign," campaign manager Robert Kennedy told them. Those scolded could not have confused Bobby with Mickey Mouse. Bobby drove his staff hard, pushed them to work long, grinding hours. Only Bobby's pushing himself harder than his staff kept it from open rebellion. Robert reached peaks of intensity during campaigns that surpassed any other work he did. Nothing would get in his way to elect his brother president.

Every national campaign gets tangled in a baroque construction of wards and precincts; local politicians are eager to use whatever authority they have to wrest from the national candidate every concession they believe their due. Robert disliked this part of the process and dealt rigidly with its practitioners. He left a trail of resentment that his brother, safely above it all, could disavow. Yet both brothers were too shrewd to kill any votes because of their personal likes and dislikes. Every vote counted in this election, one of the closest races in the country's history. Robert had the job of telling patronage seekers yes or no. He could not afford to be ruthless with the local politicians that truly counted.

As with the 1952 campaign for senator, Jack Kennedy got all the praise, while Robert got all the blame. In the crucial West Virginia primary that pitted Senator Hubert H. Humphrey, a Protestant from Minnesota, against the urban, Irish Roman Catholic, Jack Kennedy needed to prove he could get non-Catholic votes. No Catholic had been elected president until 1960 and the media was full of anti-Catholic rhetoric and debate about the dual allegiances many thought Catholics had between pope and country. The primary got negative very quickly and reached the level of questioning Humphrey's war record (he had legitimate health exemptions that kept him out of service). The well-known war hero, captain of PT-109 did not get the blame, his brother did (along with FDR's son, Franklin D. Roosevelt Jr., who was enlisted to bring up the issue by the campaign). Robert played the role of dirty-trickster, at least the Humphrey campaign believed, that included disruption of Humphrey meetings and handing out anti-Catholic literature while implying it came from the Minnesotan's camp. It was the "devil" brother[15] arranging the rough tactics, not the gracious candidate. Massachusetts Governor Paul Dever was snookered in the same fashion.

We may never know the "truth" of the events leading up to the acceptance by Lyndon B. Johnson to be nominated as the Democratic vice presidential candidate. It is truly a Rashomon event. We know how it ended: with a bitter Johnson accepting the nomination and a political feud that continued until it exploded the 1968 campaign for president. Bobby's ruthless reputation hardened forever in the hotel suites of the Los Angeles Democratic Convention.

Robert Kennedy lamented that with Jack's nomination, the campaign had only twenty-four hours to select a vice presidential running mate. While technically accurate, and the Kennedy campaign was probably so involved in winning delegate support at the convention that they indeed had no time seriously to consider a running mate, Jack Kennedy must have discussed who he would nominate for vice president over the long months of the primary campaign. The campaign had one day to make the announcement, but over a year to ruminate over who they wanted to run with against the Republican candidate, who was expected to be, and indeed was, Richard M. Nixon.

The delegates were not technically obligated to accept their presidential candidate's choice for vice president, but by custom they relied on their newly-selected candidate. So the Kennedy campaign made a hasty choice. It turned out to be one of the most tumultuous days of that year. Jack Kennedy had not truly wanted Johnson as a running mate. The liberals of the Democratic Party and its union supporters would, and did, loudly protest the choice. Labor especially resented backing someone who voted for the Taft-Hartley Act, a bill limiting union activity, passed several years before.

Robert Kennedy contended that Jack made the offer to Johnson without believing the majority leader of the senate would give up that powerful position for the relatively unheralded and weak office of vice president. Johnson had, in various degrees of openness, sought the nomination for president against Kennedy during the primary and a residue of bitterness hung between the men. So it could have been a surprise when Johnson did accept Jack Kennedy's offer. When the news reached close Kennedy aides and supporters, they exploded. They felt betrayed. Johnson's reputation was anything but liberal; they and union support would be crucial to Kennedy's chances in the fall. Kennedy faced a full revolt. If Jack truly thought Johnson would refuse, he miscalculated. It was ultimately up to Robert to play the "bad Kennedy" role, again, and try to ease Johnson out of the nomination.

Bobby visited the Johnson hotel suite three times after Jack offered the vice president's spot to the Texan politician. He openly discussed the campaign's dilemma with Johnson and his advisors in each of the three visits. Johnson was offered chairmanship of the Democratic Party. In that role, he could spend the next four to eight years dispensing patronage, putting his people in key roles in the Democratic Party. He could build a powerful base from which to run for president after Kennedy.

The crucial visit was the third one. By then, many phone calls had been traded among the two rival camps and Jack Kennedy and Johnson had talked on the phone several times. Johnson remained the choice for vice president. In what seemed like a last-ditch effort, after Jack assured him he was his choice,

Robert visited Johnson a third time to see if LBJ would relent and allow Kennedy to select another person to be vice president. Johnson and his entourage believed Robert acted, ruthlessly, on his own. Jack told Johnson that "Bobby was out of touch" and that Johnson was certainly his final and firm choice. Robert left the room and Johnson publicly announced acceptance as Jack Kennedy's running mate.

That it was a final effort to ease Johnson off the ticket is certain. However, it is highly unlikely that Robert Kennedy was acting without his brother's knowledge. Like he had done with Massachusetts Governor Paul Dever in 1952, and more recently in the West Virginia primary, it is more likely Jack wanted his brother to act in a way so he could disavow any knowledge of Bobby's actions. Whatever Robert Kennedy was, he was not a "loose canon." Jack trusted his brother to make many decisions, something as crucial as a vice presidential nomination would not be left solely up to his younger brother. As Robert later said: "I wasn't going down to see if he would withdraw just as lark on my own: 'My brother's asleep, so I'll go see if I can get rid of his vice president . . .'" Johnson never believed this. He underestimated Jack's, and overestimated Robert's, ruthlessness.

Robert arrived late to a dinner sponsored by the Women's National Press Club. Press photographers were around as his wife Ethel rushed up to greet her husband and give him a kiss. He held her off at arm's length. Jackie Kennedy noticed her sister-in-law's evident discomfort and walked over to embrace her. Lyndon Johnson was there, too. Not wanting to miss a chance to upstage his bitter foe, he walked up to Ethel and kissed her "loudly" on her cheek.[16] Lyndon Johnson had little hesitancy to make lavish public, emotional displays. Robert remained uncomfortable in public throughout his life. It would surprise journalists that Bobby never lost that fear of public intimacy that many politicians develop. One journalist noted:

> It had shaken me. I had arrived from England [in 1966] expecting to meet someone buoyant and extroverted, and had found instead someone intense and even more wary, on that first occasion at his home, than I felt myself on foreign soil.[17]

Yet we have other, opposite, accounts of Kennedy's personality. Six months after his brother's death, *The Washington Post* reporter Ben Bradlee accompanied Kennedy to a trip to a Catholic Home for the Aged in Kansas City. They found a woman there who would be dead within thirty-six hours. She lay moaning. "The death rattle already catching at her throat," Bradlee noted, she could not recognize who the people near her were or who she was. Kennedy took her hand and held it for what seemed like a long time. Bradlee thought Kennedy's physical contact with her was the only thing the woman could still understand.[18]

> He was just giving her love—non-verbal communication. It was the most poignant thing I've ever seen and I don't move easy.

Time and time again stories like this one have been told about Kennedy's amazing amount of sympathy for people in simple, one-to-one human encounters. On one of his many trips, Bobby picked up a starving boy, who had wide open wounds, without fear or repugnance, rubbing the boy's extended belly while everyone else tried just to keep the nausea down. He walked into places others would not go, as when he visited Brazil and the security police left him alone, when he knelt to talk to children, because the smell of the streets, foul with open sewage, was too much for the others to bear. Of course these scenes were about politics. Yet other politicians would not step into such situations. These visits to ghettos, migrant labor camps and hospitals went beyond the usual "photo-ops" other politicians regularly use. Nor should anyone accuse Robert Kennedy of having been a saint; he was not. Most politicians could understand issues in the abstract, read about the "other America" and let their intellect work toward a solution. Kennedy seemed to need a physical connection to his causes. Touch and smell made as much an impact on Kennedy as just reading or hearing about the wretched conditions of a coal mine, maybe more.

> If one of you guys [reporters] writes one more time about his looking like a choirboy, I'll kill you. A choirboy is sweet, soft, cherubic. Take a look at that bony little face, those hard, opaque eyes, and then listen to him bawl somebody out. Some choirboy![19]

That statement came from a state department employee during the Kennedy administration who had just suffered an attack by Robert. The seeming dichotomy between the ruthless Bobby and the sensitive one evaporates when one considers that the complaints of ruthlessness usually came from politicians, government employees and other people whom Kennedy saw as having sufficient rank. Rarely does one find stories of campaign volunteers or soup kitchen workers noting a mean streak in the man. A Justice Department attorney whom Kennedy believed ill-prepared, presidential advisors whom Kennedy collared and jabbed fingers at while belittling their loyalty to President Kennedy, campaign staff members who complained about the grueling pace set by the campaign manager, all complained vehemently and all considered Robert Kennedy ruthless, a son of a bitch. "Oh, bullshit. Everybody bitches about Bobby and I'm getting sick and Goddamn tired of it," said Jack Kennedy. "He's the only one who doesn't stick knives in my back, the only one I can count on when it comes down to it."[20]

Such loyalty does not exist in the truly ruthless. Robert Kennedy drove his people hard, it is true, but there was more of Henry the V in him than Richard the III. Robert Kennedy understood the advice Nick Carraway received from his father in *The Great Gatsby*: Bobby knew all the people in the world did not possess his advantages. Those with advantages he challenged, like the university students complaining about the Vietnam War while safe behind their college deferments. When he met his equals, in competition or cooperation, he drove them as hard as he drove himself. People of sufficient rank he bullied and badgered when they fell short of his expectations. And when he met people who were disadvantaged, those who could not sufficiently overcome personal hardships and who lacked social approval, he reached out to help.

If that was ruthless, it was a splendid ruthlessness.

4

Terrible Honesty

We must soften into a credulity below the milkiness of infancy to think all men virtuous. We must be tainted with a malignancy truly diabolical, to believe all the world to be equally wicked and corrupt.

—Edmund Burk

NOBODY CONFUSED JOSEPH F. GLIMCO with an honest union leader. The president of Chicago's Teamsters Local 777 had been arrested many times, but never convicted up to the time he testified before the Senate Permanent Subcommittee on Investigations or the McClellan committee (chaired by Senator John L. McClellan, D-Arkansas). That did not stop young Senate Counsel Robert Kennedy. He persisted in making incriminating statements, forming them as questions, and then asking Glimco to agree with him. Glimco consistently refused on the grounds that the answers he gave under oath in a senate chamber could incriminate him in a court of law. In short, he pleaded the Fifth, over and over again.

"I respectfully decline to answer because I honestly believe my answer might tend to incriminate me," Glimco replied to a Kennedy statement/question.

"I would agree with you," Kennedy said.

"I respectfully decline . . ." Glimco tried to reiterate until Kennedy cut him off.

"You haven't got the guts to [answer], have you, Mr. Glimco?"

Joseph P. Kennedy congratulating his son Robert, who served as a
seaman second class on the destroyer *Joseph P. Kennedy Jr.*
(John F. Kennedy Library and Museum)

That's when committee chairman McClellan chimed in: "Morally you are kind of yellow inside, are you not? That is the truth about it?"

"Fifth Amendment."

The complexity of trying to define Robert Kennedy is no more evident than in his work as senate counsel for the McClellan committee, investigating corrupt unions, gangsters and Jimmy Hoffa. Such a collection of hoods, thieves, bribe takers and givers, leg breakers and murderers had never been seen by an American audience. That was the point. Like Joseph McCarthy and Roy Cohn before him, McClellan and Kennedy's aims were precisely to publicize the danger of "the enemy within" and hope that through this exposure American law enforcement could break up organized crime.

Before the cameras and microphones, the "witnesses" had no chance to cross examine or to access an impartial judge. While the courts have long decided that the right to refuse to answer due to risk of self-incrimination extends to a legislative hearing, those testifying must appear in answer to a Congressional subpoena. In court, an accused person need not testify at all. Thus, legislators can simply force a witness to repeat their right to avoid self-incrimination over and over if they want to make the witness appear to be uncooperative or guilty. Instead of being a pillar of our law and democratic institutions, pleading the Fifth has been popularized as a technicality resorted to by the guilty and only the guilty.

The McClellan committee heard testimony from over fifteen hundred witnesses. About one fifth of them "took the Fifth" instead of directly answering questions of counsel and committee members. Kennedy said very few of those "in my estimation were free of wrongdoing." He also wrote that most of the people who took the Fifth on every request did so "when the facts had already been established in the record or when I had some definite information to support the question."[1] In other words, he questioned those who took the Fifth even though he already knew the answers, or thought he did, and so did not necessarily need the testimony. Kennedy wanted to solve problems, get to the ends with less care about the means than republics or democracies demand. He admitted that all the evidence was not fully proven. "I am not claiming that when I questioned a witness I always had positive proof on the subject . . . In many instances, where a gangster was concerned, the information came from police files and could not be positively verified."[2]

Congressional hearings afford few protections that courts have available to defendants. Technically, those hauled before a committee are not defendants, and the history of such hearings show the potential for praise as well as abuse. We trust the moral character of our legislators to be responsible, but the only safeguard against abuse—publicity—is in itself the goal of those who would purposefully use hearings for malevolent ends.

Kennedy noted in his book about the hearings, *The Enemy Within*, that he had worked for Senator Joseph McCarthy, but found the ardent anti-Communist's methods repugnant. He said his committee's work differed in that the McCarthy committee did no real research so it was never able to check its "pet theories." To prevent such abuse, Kennedy wrote, committees should do sound investigative work before they present cases. His staff strove to present evidence that would be admissible in a court of law, Kennedy said, but because the committee's goal was legislation and not indictments, it was not bound by strict rules of evidence and did, admittedly, introduce hearsay testimony. Luckily, Robert Kennedy remained honest and avoided more terrible miscarriages of justice and moral abuse. However, berating witnesses over and over for availing themselves of constitutional protections abuses the spirit of the Fifth Amendment. The goal of writing legislation to stop corruption and organized crime was paramount in Kennedy's mind. The process became secondary.

Kennedy was staunchly anti-Communist and conservative as he entered public life. He also was a true believer in God and adhered closely to his Roman Catholic faith. Because of this, his investigative zeal against crooked unions and gangsters often gets assigned to his simple religious view of good and evil. While he may have seen many of the people brought to witness in the senate as "evil," and himself on the side of the good, the decision to fight against the "rackets" looks more a practical political decision than a simplistic moral one. Kennedy was sophisticated enough and experienced through his association with the McCarthy committee to see how forcefully a senate investigation could project its participants into national fame. A senate investigation that was more thorough and honest, but that had similar national import, would succeed where McCarthy failed.

No more explosive headlines could have been written, or national coverage given, than for a crusade against organized crooks. Kennedy must have seen the endless possibilities of bringing gangsters to national attention. The stories would be dramatic, colorful and entertaining. It was an issue that could end in serving the public good and his private moral vision. He could gain a reputation apart from his brother and he could be at the forefront of an important issue of his times.

This was not the quest of a religious zealot nor a man who saw the world in simple dichotomies. Hardball politics underlay the decision to bring this national corruption to the surface. Was Kennedy enigmatic and divided? At times he was. But as much as any political figure of his times, Kennedy knew himself and steered his public life so that it did not drastically conflict with his private beliefs. Nothing fit the bill better than fighting gangsters. The pragmatic politician investigated corruption, not the altar boy.

Taking the Fifth

Over the entrance to Harvard Law School are the words "Non sub Homine sed sub Deo et Lege," Not under men, but under God and the law. Maybe if Kennedy had attended Harvard Law he would have better appreciated the concept.

Kennedy added to the Fifth Amendment's smarmy reputation during his time as counsel to the McClellan committee. That availing oneself of the Fifth is often seen as a refuge for scoundrels is part of the legacy Kennedy shares with Senator Joseph McCarthy's investigations of the Communist threat. The investigative tactic was (and is) simple: if a suspected lawbreaker is asked in open committee hearings, especially if televised, what seem to be reasonable questions over and over, and each time replies with his constitutional right to not reply for fear of self-incrimination (taking the Fifth) the person under questioning becomes a person of questionable character.

A defendant in a court of law has the right not to testify on his own behalf; if the defendant testifies, he waives his Fifth Amendment right and must answer relevant questions. A person called to testify in front of a legislative committee is more vulnerable since the testimony is compelled. The courts have long recognized this dilemma and the Fifth Amendment privilege has been interpreted to be comprehensive in its application. So even if the person testifying in front of a legislative investigation can pick and choose which questions to answer, witnesses before Congress have no Fifth Amend-

ment right not to show up. That gives prosecutorial-leaning legislative counsels a great advantage.

"If we are not willing to let the Amendment be invoked, where, over time, are we going to stop when police, prosecutors, or chairmen want to get people to talk? Lurking in the background here are really ugly dangers which might transform our whole system of free government," wrote constitutional scholar Erwin N. Griswold in *The Fifth Today*. Griswold noted that congressional committees are not the place to find the highest standards of Constitutional protection.

If congressional committees remain honest, forthright and above reproach, they are especially tempted to use their subpoena authority to compel testimony unwisely, since they may not recognized their own abuse of authority. When this subpoena power is abused, only those who are the subject or close to the subject of the investigation complain.

Unfortunately, Kennedy in his zeal used the McClellan committee specifically to expose people he decided were gangsters. Unlike McCarthy, however, he did not tarnish people without first thoroughly doing the groundwork to assure himself, at least, and the investigative staff that those targeted were indeed "bad guys." His intentions were honest and he believed in his personal integrity. This is of little constitutional comfort. We have no way to check this power of government according to the character of the investigators.

Had he survived, Robert Kennedy would be nine months older
than Fidel Castro is today. That Castro survived is not due to the
actions of either Robert or Jack Kennedy, or at least that is what
many people today believe. Robert claimed he stopped the assassination plots against Castro. No known documents directly link
Castro assassination plots with either Kennedy. Only circum-
stantial evidence links Jack and Robert to the Castro plots.
Neither Kennedy would have put such an order in writing; no
president would want a record of an assassination order to surface. Thousands of documents remain classified or unreleased
by the Kennedy family. Final answers may lie there. More likely
there is no smoking gun. Neither Kennedy is likely to have plotted to murder Castro.

America has been obsessed with Fidel Castro from the
moment his revolution succeeded. He has survived through nine
presidential administrations in over more than four decades of
rule. The best (or worst, depending on how you look at it) efforts
of American intelligence, military and foreign policy efforts have
failed to dislodge him. Castro has even survived the downfall of
the Soviet Union, the country that subsidized the Caribbean
Communist country and helped keep it financially viable while
America has isolated Cuba with economic embargo.

No administration had Cuba more on its mind than Jack
Kennedy's. From the failed Bay of Pigs invasion in 1961 to his
very own assassination, Castro and his revolution inextricably
intertwined with the New Frontier. When the Soviets put offensive missiles in Cuba, it ignited a crises that put the world closer to nuclear war than it has been before or since. The Kennedys
became obsessed with Castro. Robert the ardent anti-
Communist put intense pressure on the CIA to do something
about Cuba. It had been before Jack Kennedy become president

and continued to try to do something about the Cuban dictator after Kennedy became president: murder him.

There is no doubt the American government planned the assassination of Castro. Members of the CIA began operations they hoped would lead to Castro's death late in the Eisenhower administration. It contemplated putting thallium salts in his shoes, hoping to make his beard fall out. Another plan had cigars laced with a special chemical to disorientate Castro; another cigar plan put botulinum in cigars destined for Castro's mouth. It even hired members of organized crime, in the fall of 1960, evidently hoping professional killers would better do the dirty deed than American agents. They failed miserably, too.

CIA and other intelligence officials cite the atmosphere created by the Kennedys, particularly the pressure Robert Kennedy put on the agency to do something about Castro. With the amount of pressure so high, many people believe Jack or Robert Kennedy did not need to directly order the death of Castro. Such tasks get approved without written or recorded assents to keep a up level of plausible deniability if the plots are ever revealed. Trouble with that argument is that plausible deniability also advantages those covert operators who act independently of executive control. Presidents do not have absolute control of covert or even overt operations. During the Cuban missile crisis, for example, President Kennedy found out a general had ordered a high level of alert and did not consult nor ask for presidential permission. Each president must learn for himself how to bring military and intelligence forces under control. They are part of an on-going government that reigns before and after presidents come and go. Sometimes, when these military officials and intelligence bureaucrats stay in power too long, they believe they have the authority to act outside civilian control.

It is unlikely either Kennedy would have countenanced murder. First of all, the risks of revelation were frighteningly high. President Kennedy learned early in his term that secrets are difficult, if not impossible, to keep. His personal intervention with *The New York Times* kept that newspaper from printing the details of the Cuban invasion—barely. Had it found out that a plot to assassinate a foreign leader was real, *The Times* or any other newspaper would not "spike" the story.

Public revelation would not have been the more serious issue. If the Soviets found out, and could prove that President Kennedy planned to kill Castro, their restraint in Western Europe, especially in Berlin, would evaporate. President Kennedy was more cognizant of the wider conflict such reckless behavior would spark than any real threat posed by the island of Cuba. Such restraint kept him from ordering immediate military strikes against the missiles placed in Cuba in 1962 by the Soviets. Had Premier Khrushchev been given smoking-gun evidence of America's plans to overthrow or kill Castro, America's credibility could have been damaged enough to allow its nuclear weapons a home in the Caribbean.

President Kennedy was a shrewd gamesman; there is little evidence he was reckless. Except for the Bay of Pigs fiasco, Jack Kennedy always sought negotiation and mutual accommodation. Furthermore, he was shrewd enough a politician to know plausible deniability makes no sense. Blame rises to the top. He would be blamed no matter if the order came directly from him, his brother or if the act was done by a super-secret covert operation.

The only serious threat Castro posed to the Kennedy administration involved domestic American politics. Conservative and radical right-wing politicians put up an even fiercer front against Cuban communism than the attorney general. Many people demanded the United States take over the island—regardless of the presence of Soviet missiles—and remove Castro immediately. That an island of six million people, which survived only with the economic assistance of the Soviet Union, posed so great a threat to the world strained credulity, and President Kennedy probably understood that and would have been highly reluctant to start an international incident over Cuba.

The burden of proof lies with the accusers; if the evidence exists, they need to find it. Few Washington secrets have had the unrevealed forty-year half-life of the alleged Kennedy plot against Castro. So far, only a complex web of innuendo links the president and his brother to any such action. If presidents order assassinations, they do it with a gesture, a nod of the head, argue the proponents of the Castro assassination story. This would be a most lethal, highly-honed, non-verbal skill.

It all seemed so exciting, then. They would wear special berets, green, and could quickly get in, do their job, and quickly get out. Robert invited members of the special unit to Hyannis Port to demonstrate their techniques. Waging guerrilla war was not its intent; preventing it was more the goal. "Counterinsurgency might best be described as social reform under pressure," wrote Robert Kennedy. A memo went to General Maxwell Taylor on December 7, 1961. It discussed:

> exploiting the potential of the underworld in Cuban cities to harass and bleed the Communist control apparatus. This effort may, on a very sensitive basis, enlist the assistance of American links to the Cuban underworld. While this would be a CIA project, close cooperation of the FBI is imperative.[3]

American harassment of Cuba under the oversight of Robert Kennedy included blowing up bridges, burning fields of sugar cane, blowing up mines, disrupting power supplies and the like. These practices were called sabotage in another era and what we

Robert and Jack Kennedy during the McClellan committee hearings.
(© *Look* (Jones))

would describe today, if practiced by outside forces or domestic radical groups against America, as terrorism.

A special task force was setup: Special Group (Augmented), whose aim was the overthrow of the Castro government. "No money, effort or manpower is to be spared" to destroy the Cuban government, Robert told the members of this special team. "Presidential staffers talked about how Robert Kennedy was 'out-CIAing the CIA.' He became, in Thomas Power's words, a 'haunting presence' over the CIA."[4] As President Kennedy hoped he would be. After the Bay of Pigs, Jack rued the appointment of his brother to head the Department of Justice. Robert was more needed to watch over the intelligence agency where his absolute loyalty would serve the president better than in Justice. The CIA's largest budget item of the time was for Operation Mongoose, the program designed to cause domestic havoc in Cuba and whose creation and operation Robert oversaw.

The climate of the early 1960s was blisteringly anti-Castro, inside the administration and in Congress. Just after the Bay of Pigs, with Robert overseeing a National Security Council meeting, he began to rail against State Department reports that found Castro was firmly, immovably, entrenched in power.

> This is worthless. What can we do about Cuba? This doesn't tell us anything . . . You people are so anxious to protect your own asses that you're afraid to do anything. All you want to do is dump the whole thing on the president.

The anti-Cuba, anti-Castro atmosphere touched many parts of American society; economic interest in what was essentially a United State colony for most the century ran deep. Not only did Cuban exiles lose property and investments when the revolution deposed Zaldívar Batista, dozens of American corporations had stakes in the country as did organized crime, which nearly overnight lost a very lucrative source of income from gambling and prostitution. Anti-Communist rhetoric continued to taint nearly every foreign policy discussion through the Kennedy years; the end of the McCarthy era only heightened the American obsession with the destruction of Communist governments.

Liberal and middle-of-the-road politicians ignored the conservative pressure against Castro if they wanted to lose elections. Public opinion and political rhetoric was so over-whelmingly arraigned to destroy the Castro government, the logical leap needed by military and intelligence officials to destroy Castro himself was a short step. Cuba's threat to American homogeny in the region had been exaggerated. Despite its support of other Latin American revolutionary movements, and the example it set for those movements, a country as dependent on the Soviets for its economic survival posed little real threat to the United States.

The truth is, except for the prestige and its image in the rest of the world, Cuba was of little value to the Soviets. It remained a net drain to the USSR's budget and offered little strategic interest. Like West Berlin to the United States, the USSR would have had to defend the island country in some way, but reluctantly. America's conventional military strength in the Caribbean was overwhelming. Only a nuclear strategy would have been available to the Soviets if they wished to gain a stronger foothold in the region.

Any American president in office during the early 1960s would have to put up a strong front against Cuba. Jack Kennedy's small electoral mandate guaranteed his administration would have to support a strong anti-Cuban policy. Not only would his reelection depend on it, Democratic control of the Congress in the 1962 elections was threatened. Add to that an attorney general who had a strong anti-Communist personal and public history, one who was fully enthusiastic about covert operations in other countries, and you end up with a climate that could support assassination schemes and outright military intervention, even if those policies proved misguided and ultimately futile. The State Department report Robert Kennedy so vehemently derided, now in hindsight, proved correct. Castro has showed the world he is resilient and irresolute. That he survived so long, particularly after the fall of the USSR and its annual infusions of cash into the Cuban economy, demonstrates how correct the State Department was in its 1961 report.

The Kennedys' initiatives, Robert Kennedy's support of covert programs of coercion and sabotage, were its and his worst public policy decisions. Not only did they completely fail to dislodge Castro and communism from Cuba, the cost was staggering and the waste of energies enormous. An earlier accommodation with Castro may have showed a better result than forty years of stalemate. Robert Kennedy's success at gaining release of the Cuban prisoners, negotiations for whom continued even through the Cuban missile crisis, showed some basis of negotiation with the Communist regime was possible.

The American aggressive political climate could not support any form of outreach to Cuba except hostile, anti-Communist rhetoric. This ensured decades of blundering Cuban policies. The Kennedys set the tone of American hostility to Cuba that continues to keep the two countries sadly at odds when most of the reasons for hostility have waned.

In his first speech as attorney general, Robert Kennedy addressed the University of Georgia Law School, in the spring of 1961, after the federal court ordered two black students the right to entry. Unpopular as that decision was, and as unpopular as any federal official's appearance just after the two students enrolled, Kennedy was adamant about giving the school's law day address. It set the tone for the administration's civil rights policies over the next two and half years, one that would try to allow for local social customs and not lead the charge to change Southern life with Northern standards. But he did emphasize the rule of law and that his Justice Department was ready to enforce the law at any time. Asserting his personal belief in the correctness of civil rights, Robert Kennedy went on to assert that no matter his personal belief, the court ruling allowing the two black students into the university would be enforced. It signaled what would lie ahead.

The curious part of the speech was its opening, that posed two areas that were his obsessions during the 1950s: the "rackets" and the threat to the free enterprise system by "our enemies" or Communists. He blended a cynical America willing to see everything as "a racket" and an America that can set itself as an example to the rest of the world by providing justice and "the rule of law." Civil rights especially would show countries teetering on the brink of communism how better the American system can be. The fight for civil rights became in his eyes another tool in the Cold War.

Since it was early in the administration, Kennedy needed to signal what his department would be focusing on in the months and years ahead. A single-issue speech would give that issue, albeit an important one such as civil rights, an unwanted emphasis. The overall emphasis was on "the rule of law." Over and over, poking the dais for emphasis, Kennedy reaffirmed that court rulings would be enforced and warned against the use of violence. He praised local officials who would work with the Department of Justice to keep the peace in their localities. The plight of the previous administration over whether to send federal troops to enforce desegregation rulings weighed on the new attorney general who understood how quickly an uncontrolled local outburst could destroy the reputation of his brother's presidency.

The Kennedy administration did more for civil rights than any since the Civil War. Many black leaders acknowledged the Kennedys' role in forcing Southern schools and public facilities to integrate. Attorney General Robert Kennedy took an active part in bringing blacks into prominent jobs within his department. Still, he appointed some federal judges who were outright hostile to the civil rights movement. Robert believed black leaders would understand his political dilemma. Some leaders understood; but some black leaders thought Kennedy needed to understand their plight better.

Robert Kennedy would face a roomful of black social and political leaders two years after that Georgia Law school speech. They would lash into him and bitterly complain that the pace of achieving equal opportunity for blacks was too slow and the rage was about to explode. As angry as he was at that time about the confrontation, feeling that he was "set up," Kennedy would go on to face other such confrontations, even until the last days of his 1968 presidential campaign. He would be able to shrug off such encounters, after finally realizing the need for the rage and anger to be released and he was willing to be the focus of the vitriol.

But in Athens, Georgia May 1961 Kennedy continued to be obsessed with the threat of organized crime and communism. These twin preoccupations lead to his two greatest follies: his short concern with the Fifth Amendment and the anti-Communist atmosphere that at least gave his intelligence agencies the belief that they could plot the assassination of a leader of a foreign government. It was ironic that he could so forcefully argue for the rule of law while initiating violations of Cuban sovereignty.

Malcolm X noted that the assassination of President Kennedy

was a case of "chickens coming home to roost." What would happen at home in America, through the long years of violence in the streets by blacks and Vietnam War protesters, was a continuation of violence condoned by United States leaders plotting warlike foreign policies. Robert Kennedy preached sermons of peace and anti-violence (especially after the assassination of the Reverend Martin Luther King Jr.). Yet his actions while overseeing the CIA and American covert operations followed another path, one that condoned terrorism in the name of ending Communist rule. He should take his part of the blame for the atmosphere of American violence that ensued.

Senator Robert F. Kennedy speaking in New York City.
(© Burt Berinsky)

5

Demagogue

There are only two things that get into your blood
politics and the motion picture business."
–Robert F. Kennedy

ROBERT KENNEDY WAS THE FIRST pin-up politician. Other politicians could become popular; Kennedy ran for president as a celebrity. His image sold right alongside Marlon Brando's decked out in his "Wild Bunch" outfit and Marilyn Monroe's uncontrollable dress in the poster shops. Celebrity greeted him at each public appearance. The crowds dangerously pushed as close as they could to shake his hand, touch his hair, to grab any part of him. Some people believe he flirted with demagoguery. Maybe. It is also true that Kennedy ran for president at a time politics was evolving into entertainment.

The new style politics practiced by the Kennedy brothers, the fresh, young faces that embittered "last hurrah" politicians (like the old Boston pols of the 1950s), was already aging by the time Bobby ran for president. By the time he ran, Bobby had to have been outfitted with a new character, one sized for the era of change and dissent. Like no other politician before him, not even as one so savvy as Jack Kennedy, Robert was on the vanguard of a new breed of politician. He was a celebrity of the people, a "celebergogue."

Creating a character, building a story around a politician, is older than American politics. All presidents have relied on an image to represent themselves to the electorate. President Kennedy acted out a dramatic story: the war hero, scholar, man of courage and action. He exemplified youth and rugged health (at the same time he suffered physically like no other president from a variety of physical ills). Despite the glamour built around him as America's celebrity-president, he ruled conventionally compared to today's media-contained environment. The images of Kennedy children playing in the Oval Office look quaint next to the finely-honed images that travel with candidates today.

Bobby had his own story, modeled on Jack's, complete with his Roosevelt-era initials (FDR, JFK, LBJ, RFK), signature idealistic quote ("But I dream things that never were and say 'Why not?' "), books written under his name and the Kennedy chic. That is not to say Robert Kennedy cynically exploited the death of his brother. He evoked Jack Kennedy's memory; to be sure, he merely had to show up to do that. What worked for Jack could work for Bobby and the borrowed bits of character worked exceedingly well.

Far more poignant than anything anyone could purposely muster, Kennedy walked with a deep, undeniable, tragic air after his brother's death. We want our heroes to have a sense of tragedy; it makes their struggles epic and thus more vivid. The tragedy that befell Robert Kennedy changed forever the political, public man into mythic hero. If his brother charmed his way into American hearts, Robert's personal tragedies sunk him into the deepest crevices of our psyches.

He was easily demonized, too. There is no denying that Robert Kennedy touched those that hated him as deeply as those who loved him. The reaction to RFK depends on how you look at politics; people tended to love or hate him. Ambivalence answers the cautious politician, fascination the passionate one.

There was no turning away. Kennedy relished in the physical exertion and the power of the crowd. Part of this was the pragmatic politician in him. Especially in 1968, he had to show as much popular support to the Democratic power brokers as needed to win him the nomination. The other part of him relished the adulation. If he could be as hated as he was constantly reminded in the press, the crowds could love him as they did and dispel the unpleasant taste left from the ruthless image that dogged him all his adult life. His brother taught him a great deal about statesmanship and being the gamesman. The more important lessen taught Robert was how to be a showman. Robert learned quickly. He could have taught his brother a thing or two about being a star.

"He had no obvious leadership qualities—no charisma," said a classmate of his from the University of Virginia Law School. "He's not an Adam Clayton Powell who can walk into a courtroom and dominate it."[1]

How does one account, then, for Truman Capote's description of his United National Plaza neighbor, that Kennedy could make people jump?

> Meaning, if you move through a room and everything is galvanized on you and you're terribly aware of it, and people . . . move out of their way to make room for you . . . in effect, they 'jump.' I think Bobby had that power, but he rarely used it.[2]

Like everything else Kennedy did, he worked hard at it. If he was a poor study, he worked twice as hard as anyone else would. That he could become president added to allure. His early social awkwardness worked against his later charisma.

Kennedy looked awful in his 1964 senate campaign commercials. Nothing his campaign handlers could do helped him look anything but uncomfortable in television ads. Then in the first week of October, at Columbia University, Kennedy spent two hours with a group of students. The encounter was entirely antagonistic. However, when the tapes were viewed, the campaign people knew they had winning film. "Bobby laughing at the abuse and razor-sharp in his replies." They ran a half hour of the tape in paid, prime-time television and cut it up into thirty-second spots. From then on, a film crew followed the senate candidate and fed unedited tape to local television news stations.[3] Live and raw Robert Kennedy had TV appeal. While the entire political ethos was heading in the other direction—tightly controlled conditions, nothing but scripted replies to scripted questions—Kennedy live played well.

The very medium that helped cement a hard reputation of the tough prosecutor now portrayed a feisty, dynamic activist. Kennedy lived up to the role and then some. In every way he could he foisted the image of rapid shooting, mountain climbing, man of action, a feisty debater who could take the devil's advocate role with relish. When Robert Kennedy came to town, whether it was to put the spotlight on the horrible conditions suffered by coal miners in South America or to challenge the true commitment of anti-war students protected by college deferment from the draft, you could bet there would be fireworks. He not only played to the camera, he lived the role of a man of action.

A coast guard cutter approached a schooner off the coast of Long Island in September 1965. Thirty knot winds buffeted the water. Bobby was aboard the sailboat with his wife and a friend. The cutter came to tell the Kennedys their daughter Kathleen had suffered head injuries at a horse show. Rather than risk the

Coast Guard ship smashing the schooner in the ten-foot waves, Kennedy dove in and swam fifty yards to the cutter. He plunged into even more dangerous waters in Colorado while rafting through rapids. Off the coast of Maine, he jumped into the ocean to save his dog Freckles. He kayaked down the Salmon River and skied to the brink of endurance on steep slopes. He often displayed physical bravado before reporters and cameras, but he acted no differently when they were not looking.

Kennedy would have been more comfortable on the "Wide World of Sports" than he looked on "Face the Nation." It showed. So as Kennedy's advisors began to gain more insight into their man, his popularity grew. People saw in his face his brother's face, heard his brother's voice in his voice—at first. More and more, as 1963 began to fade into the tragic years of Vietnam, inner city riots and general dissolution, Robert forged his own persona, headline by headline, speech by speech, confrontation by confrontation. And the anticipation grew that this third Kennedy son would ascend to the presidency.

"I'm scared [of death], but I'm not *scared* scared," Kennedy told an interviewer. "I play Russian roulette every time I get up in the morning, but I just don't care—there's nothing I can do about it anyway."[4]

The image of the tragic hero grew steadily in the minds of Americans and in Kennedy's own imagination.

On a South America tour, Kennedy became perturbed that he would not be allowed to speak to students at the university in Chile. Jabbing with his finger in time to his words, Kennedy angrily lectured the Communist student leaders who tried to stop him from speaking: "Fifty or sixty persons can stop a speech. I know that. I don't mind getting hit by an egg. I've been hit by worse in my career." Later, he shouted his speech to a meeting full of

Communists "where the atmosphere was not far short of violence." Kennedy could do so well in this role because he was a courageous man who excelled in physical confrontations. In this excitement something, anything, might happen. One might even expect to be around when an assassin could catch up to another Kennedy.

He almost was unable to perceive issues unless he had a physical connection. On that same South American trip, the day after the confrontation with the Communist students, he visited a coal mine. Kennedy insisted he needed to go down into the hole with the miners. The mine's manager argued with the visiting senator. "Those men are Communists, they'll kill you," the manager said to Kennedy. That did not stop him from going down into the mine and walking five miles through the tunnel until he found the workers. Would the shift superintendent be a Communist if he had to work in the mine, Kennedy wondered. He had to agree he would. "If I worked in this mine, I'd be a Communist, too," Kennedy told American reporters present.[5] Not only might he do anything, he might say anything, too.

The senate bored Kennedy, its slow pace and the gradual way a freshman member must work toward being a fully-recognized member of the club. Once, after waiting for hours to question a witness in front of a committee, Robert asked his younger brother Edward M. Kennedy (who outranked him in the senate), "Is this the way I become a good senator—sitting here and waiting for my turn?" "Yes," said Ted. Still unsatisfied, Robert continued, "How many hours do I have to sit here to be a good senator?"

"As long as necessary, Robbie."

Robert Kennedy did not like waiting. He wanted answers; he wanted policies quickly put in place; he wanted executive authority. Waiting wasted valuable time, time that could be put to better use by doing something. Passions ruled his politics, not intellectual agonizing. British journalist Margaret Laing, in her book on Kennedy that was published right around the time of his death, noted:

> For Robert, what he felt was always to be a more compelling factor, and doing something about what he felt was to become at once his greatest triumph and his greatest temptation. Sincerity can bring about its own share of delusions.

Like the young senate counsel in the 1950s, who seemed to know instinctively who was good and who was evil across the committee table, the freshman senator and the 1968 presidential candidate showed a great deal of impatience with the people who would advise him to stand back and take fuller measure of the situation before him. Kennedy as legislator seemed to know, too, what policies needed implementing, now. Robert Kennedy was a star politician, not a member of the cast. Why should his public have to wait?

Neither did he like waiting to be president. He had to hurry. Ambition underlies the reason for every politician's urge to run. Mr. Smith goes to Washington in the movies only. In life, strongly ambitious men attain the presidency and there is no doubt Kennedy was as ambitious as any of his contemporaries, but he had other reasons besides ambition.

For Kennedy, ambition mixed with an unusual amount of impatience and a sense of doom. "Somebody up there doesn't like us," Kennedy said after his brother Ted was severely injured in a 1964 plane crash. For someone with the religious faith of Robert Kennedy, it seems hard not to agree with this sentiment. Joe Jr. died in World War II, the war that nearly killed his other brother and did kill his brother-in-law William Hartington, his sister Kathleen's husband. She died just after the war and Robert watched helplessly as Jack neared death once again on a 1951 trip to Asia. His wife's parents were killed in a plane crash in 1955. One brother was assassinated and Edward barely survived a plane crash one year later. Then Ethel's brother was killed in a 1966 plane crash along with an old friend of Bobby's, Dean Markham. That he himself remained constantly under a vague but real threat of death from the enemies he made chasing mobsters and crooked union bosses (and some would say planning the assassination of foreign leaders) could only have added to his sense that he would not live long.

Quoting a White House associate, Laing told Kennedy he was a fatalist who did not let anything interfere with his fate. "Yes, I think that's right," Bobby replied.

His brother Edward did not appear to share Bobby's sense of doom, his impatience with process and time. A 1965 senate immigration bill both Kennedys supported and each promoted in his own way provides a good example. Edward carefully noted the contributions of other colleagues and the years of work it took to bring the bill forward for a vote. The other Senator Kennedy said the theme of the immigration bill, its repeal of the national origins system, was first incorporated in a bill the Justice Department brought forward: his department when he was attorney general. This was more than just taking credit for himself. The busy, results-oriented executive could not abide by the interminable process of legislating.

In another legislative comparison, Edward wanted $125 million for an anti-poverty bill in 1966. Robert sponsored a bill asking $350 million for his anti-poverty programs. His requests garnered $29 million. His younger, more collegially-minded brother's smaller initial request ended with around $60 million being approved. senators get results in different ways than presidents, or would-be presidents.[6]

The deadly trip would have had to have been carefully plotted. San Francisco is 350 miles away from Los Angeles. He did not necessarily need to go first to the ranch eighty miles outside of San Francisco. If he did go there first, the airstrip about an hour away could have been used. Or he could have driven down to Southern California and back; it was a ten-hour round-trip to and from Gilroy, the nearest large town to the Bates ranch. In any event, one or two days before he was scheduled to address the American Bar Association meeting (depending on the time and place you believe Bobby departed), the attorney general of the United States left his wife and children, his friends and their family, servants and ranch hands, went to Los Angeles and assisted in or killed Marilyn Monroe himself. We know he was back in Gilroy to attend church Sunday morning. Local newspapers recorded the Kennedys' presence in church. The FBI recorded Kennedy's schedule that weekend, sans a side trip to Southern California. Guest books from the Bates ranch and photo albums also show Kennedy with his family and hosts riding horses, swimming and playing, what else, touch football.

"The attorney general and his family were with us every minute from Friday afternoon to Monday and there is simply no physical way that he could have gone to Southern California and returned," said John Bates, a prominent California lawyer. (He turned down an offer to head the Justice Department's anti-trust division, under Robert, preferring not to move with his family to Washington, D.C.[7])

One of the most bizarre and twisted stories that have circulated about Robert Kennedy accuses him of conspiring to murder the movie actress. Only the story that puts Kennedy at the scene of Monroe's death tops it for audacity. From the 1964 publication of a pamphlet by a right-wing, anti-Communist fanatic

Robert Kennedy with Ethel and children, from left: Joseph, Robert Jr.,
Kathleen, David and Mary Courtney.
(© Lowe)

to the more recent fiasco involving the veteran investigative reporter Seymour M. Hersh, who was given forged documents by Laurence Cusack, people have been willing, aching, to believe Robert Kennedy killed the movie star. Another big name that joined the odd assortment of people who circulated Monroe murder conspiracies was Norman Mailer's, who first said in his 1973 book *Marilyn* that Kennedy might have helped to kill her or might have used government agents to kill her. Why did he write such lies? Mailer later admitted he needed the money.

Little money can be had writing Marilyn Monroe *was not* killed by either or both the Kennedys. Less can be obtained by saying Robert Kennedy had little opportunity to have an affair with Monroe and probably did not. On the other hand, a conglomerate swamp of cash can be had by the first person with clear, unmistakable evidence of a sexual liaison with Bobby and Marilyn. One could fuel a lifetime career with such evidence. We can nearly always rely on greed and vanity to entice people into revealing the misdeeds of miscreants and scalawags and even more so the crimes of the rich and famous. But it was not that greed's powerful allure failed over the years to produce evidence, nor did the vanities that fuel the desire for fame fail. There is just no evidence of a Marilyn Monroe murder by, or of an affair with, Robert Kennedy.

Even before a movie star became president, presidents had become celebrities. Silent as the man might have been, Calvin Coolidge happened to have been America's first radio president when his opening message to Congress was broadcast in 1923. Since then, presidents' lives have more and more been revealed to their constituents. Many have become as widely recognized, some more so, than movie stars as they gained increased access to radio, movies and television. Certainly more people recognized Charlie Chaplin in the 1920s than Herbert Hoover. One doubts if today any movie or television personality is more widely recognized than the American president.

With recognition, intimacy has grown. Roosevelt showed the way, cozying his voice into American parlors with "Fireside Chats." Television brought presidents into even closer contact with people to the point of absurdity: ignorance of the style of underwear or peculiar anatomical features of our presidents will not destroy the Republic.

As movie stars have long been the objects of American fantasies; presidents have also caught up. It may not have started with Robert Kennedy, but he was an early, conspicuous casualty in the "celebritization" of political figures. Not that celebrity unknowingly caught the president's brother; he sought out the popularity, used it as any politician does to gain votes and win office. The celebrity bug just came back to bite him harder than most politicians.

Movie audiences have always enjoyed stories about the sexual lives of their favorites. So, too, did the public make a fetish of how many women the Kennedys had sex with. Even if he did not, people might have created the fantasy that Jack Kennedy slept with Marilyn Monroe. Certainly the number of sexual liaisons between the two have be exaggerated as had the young president's entire sexual career been inflated. If President Kennedy had sex with as many women as had been reported and rumored, he would not have had time to sleep let alone give speeches and govern. Bobby simply got dragged into the fetish-making machine along with his brother:

> Given the prevailing ethos in the Kennedy family, where sexual prowess and promiscuity were viewed as a badge of masculinity, it strains credulity to imagine that he [Bobby] was immune to such virtually obligatory demonstrations of virility.[8]

In other words, without offering more than gossip and rumor, the argument comes down to this: he just had to, that's all. The writer goes on to say the suspicions about Bobby being involved in a plot to kill Marilyn reveals something about the Kennedys' need to gain and hold power. The argument is baffling. It makes more sense that revelations coming from "suspicions" about Kennedy tell us more about the people who invented the suspicions rather than the subject of them.

The various assembly of Kennedys, their spouses and lovers have probably sold more supermarket tabloids than any other group of celebrities, movie and soap opera stars included. Yet both Jack and Robert were serious about their public careers. Neither man needed the work, especially at the tremendous personal risks both faced. Jack's death could have understandably made Bobby shun publicity and raise his family in peace. That he risked his life to be a part of his political times showed a tremendous amount of courage. It was in his blood.

The Kennedy family at the coronation of Pope Pius XII, March 1939.
From left, Kathleen, Pat, Bobby, Jack, Rose, Joe Sr.,
Teddy, Eunice, Jean, Rosemary.
(John F. Kennedy Library and Museum)

6

The Altar Boy

In our sleep, pain which cannot forget falls drop by drop
upon the heart until, in our own despair, against our will,
comes wisdom through the awful grace of God.

–Aeschylus

THE SENATOR-ELECT SEEMED restless. He had won the New
York State race two weeks earlier and it was nearing the one-year
anniversary of his brother's death. John Seigenthaler, his admin-
istrative assistant during Robert's term as attorney general,
thought his old boss "somber and preoccupied." After putting
on his brother's leather aviator jacket, the one with the presidential seal, Robert said to Seigenthaler "let's go for a ride. I
want to go to confession." Most of the ride, he stared morosely
out of the window until he suddenly said, "Let's stop at
Arlington [National Cemetery] and look at Johnny's grave."
When they got there, the cemetery was closed, but climbed the
gate to get in. The guard saw them and Kennedy called out, "I'm
Mr. Kennedy!" They went to the grave and knelt to pray.[1]

Prayer was not politics nor pandering for Robert Kennedy. It
absorbed him as a private man, rounding out a life that might
have been stunted if not for his fidelity to the Church. He rarely
missed his devotional obligations and often visited churches to
pray when he felt the personal need. It is hard to imagine an
exclusively secular Robert Kennedy, one who did not have faith

in redemption—salvation through merit—and the powers of forgiveness. Such a Kennedy would not have engaged himself in the issues of his day. He often disagreed with the teachings of the Church, on abortion and birth control, when it came to public policy; privately, the man who fathered eleven children followed a strict code of personal religious devotion.

Robert closely observed Catholic ritual in his home and church "and found that it sustained his courage in the face of reality rather than providing any escape from reality."[2] Ethel was probably more observant than her husband.

> Like her mother-in-law Rose, she draws energy and comfort from her faith. Every religious detail is of the utmost significance and import to her. Many of her rooms contain a font of holy water, which she devotedly looks after. 'God help you if you run out of holy water,' said a former help with unconscious irony.[3]

Dual loyalties to his mother and father made this religious man choose a career of public service. "Saint Rose," as some affectionately, or deridingly, called her—depending on their point of view—insured Rose's third son would not completely fall underneath the spell of his father, whom Robert idolized. The parents believed in opposite means to educate the children. Rose won out with the girls, who all attended religious schools. Joe Sr. had more authority with his sons, and except for a couple of lapses, Robert had to follow the secular strictures of his father. Finding a compromise that must have satisfied both maternal church and fraternal piety to worldly concerns took him some time and was not fully realized until the day he announced his presidential candidacy. That may have been Robert's most successful political achievement, satisfying both the religious and secular interests of competing parents.

Finally Rose got her way and put one of her sons into a Catholic school. Portsmouth Priory school stressed Catholic religious instruction. It suited the young man, who spent much of his time learning Christian doctrine and the liturgy of the Church. Robert attended weekly sermons on spiritual and moral subjects and took part in an annual retreat during Holy Week. "I feel like a saint," wrote the fifteen-year-old boy after spending three hours of praying in chapel.[4] For all his devotion, he earned only a sixty-four in Christian doctrine. He may have felt like a saint, but he was no theologian.

Joe Sr. did not approve of the religious emphasis. He believed his son should concentrate on secular subjects. "The boy is spending far too much time on religious subjects and not enough on academics," wrote Joe Sr. "That's what will get him into Harvard, the religion won't." Robert's father was a faithful Catholic, but he told people he was anti-clerical. Yet he also noted that two of his closest friends were clerics. His convictions lay more in the direction of earthly subjects. Formal religious schooling was out for the Kennedy sons.

Rose Kennedy enrolled Robert in Priory while Ambassador Kennedy remained in England as it prepared for war with Germany. Before Portsmouth, Robert attended St. Paul's, an Episcopal prep school, which he did not like. He complained that he was forced to attend chapel and read the Protestant Bible a number of times daily. Rose complained to husband that Robert was getting too much Protestantism. Joe Sr. wanted him back in Riverdale Country Day School. Rose enrolled him in Portsmouth Priory without her husband's permission. [5]

> I wanted all the children to have at least a few years in good
> Catholic schools, where along with excellent secular educa-

tion they would receive thorough instruction in the doctrines of their religion and intelligent answers to any doubts or perplexities. A child thus educated, I maintained, would have more poise, more peace of mind, more confidence about settling the problems of everyday living, and a better concept of his duties toward his God, his neighbor, and himself.

Joe Sr. disagreed. "He said that a child learned faith and morals at home, and that for boys, in particular, when they grew up they would be dealing with people of all faiths or none, and he wanted them to meet all men on their merits without consciousness of religious factors, which were matters of personal belief."[6]

It was left to Rose to oversee the children's religious upbringing. She would take some of the children when they were young on shopping trips to local stores, remembering particularly that the local five and dime fascinated the children.

Almost always, on our way home, we stopped in at our parish church. Part of the reason was that I wanted them to understand, from early age, that church isn't just something for Sundays and special times on the calendar but should be a part of daily life.[7]

Rose did not have as much to say about her oldest boy, Joseph P. Kennedy Jr. who was entirely educated in secular schools. John and Robert spent some time in Catholic schools, with Robert spending the most time in religious schools and being the most serious about his Roman Catholic faith. "I suppose they all were alter boys," said his sister Pat Kennedy,

but [Robert] was next youngest to me and for some years there he was the little brother, who I was conscious of his ambition and how much he worked at it. My room was between his and Mother's. I used to go into his room to hear his Latin. Then Mother would come in, or he'd go into her room, so he could show her how much he'd learned. He worked hard at it.

Harris Wofford, who would serve as civil rights advisor to the Kennedy administration, said "Bobby was a little altar boy all his life."[8] His brother Jack prayed and went to church often, but he had a measure of doubt. Joe Jr. paid more attention to his spiritual beliefs, kneeling in prayer every night. Joe became president of the Holy Name Society at the naval academy in Jacksonville, Mississippi. When visiting Rome's Scala Sana or Holy Stairs opposite Lateran Palace, the eldest brother climbed the stairs on his knees. [9]

Young Robert fully accepted his religion, without speculating or analyzing. He became an altar boy at St. Joseph's Roman Catholic Church in Bronxville, the Kennedys' home parish and it is where he received his first communion in April 1933. As he grew older, Bobby did not hesitate to return to this role. As a young adult, he would volunteer to be the altar boy if, while attending mass, he saw the priest without one.

His father, though admitting his anti-clerical leaning, considered himself a faithful Catholic.[10] But the ambassador was very much a man of the world and world events: "I can hardly remember a mealtime when the conversation was not dominated by what Franklin D. Roosevelt was doing or what was happening in the world," Robert wrote about his father.

While living in England, Robert would often visit the church as the family nurse, Luella Hennessey Donovan took him and his younger brother Edward home from school. The route home took them past Brompton Oratory, where the family worshiped. Bobby would go in and pray for a few minutes, according to Luella. Also while he was still in England, young Robert heard from a church employee that the priests used their own pay to heat their rooms; if money was short, they did not have any fire. He told this to his father, who sent a year's supply of wood to the priests the next day.[11]

God did not enter Robert Kennedy's life through a moment of despair, though tragedy may have deepened his religious resolves, matured an altar boy's rote beliefs. Kennedy had a life-long devotion to his religion that did not waiver nor lessen as he grew and became the pragmatic campaign manager, administration official and a candidate himself. Its roots ran into his Irish heritage and were cultured by his mother's convictions. Robert became the most devoted to Catholicism of his siblings and to its conviction that God has a design for the universe and a place for everyone in this scheme. Many nonreligious writers have mistaken this piety for Kennedy's early stiff, rigid personality. The truth lies more in the other direction. It was religion that tempered his character and was more responsible for his identification with the poor, the powerless and other outcasts of society.

Kennedy was a true believer in the mold of his mother, tinged with the anti-clerical feelings of his father. The enigma of Robert Kennedy's character may stem from this basic clash between pleasing both mother and father. Rose Kennedy wanted a more religious upbringing for her children while Joe Sr. wanted his sons to be practical men of the world. Robert had to blend the secular with sanctity, and it dominated nearly all of his adult life. That he felt sympathy for the neglected members of our world and the need, the conviction, that he could help them, came from this blending of religious belief and secular authority.

Yet it would be a mistake to confuse his religious piety with a rigid sense of good and evil. His religion always seemed more expansive than exclusive. He became more inflexible when politics or the law was involved, but more forgiving of peoples' personal lapses. The young Cold Warrior would have more easily embraced a sudden religious conversion of a Communist enemy than a political one. His missteps came from naïve notions of world politics and lax understanding of law; the greatest triumphs were reached when he let himself be guided by his moral instincts and education.

Two weeks before Christmas in 1942, Robert Kennedy was at the Milton Academy with his friend Sam Adams when news came that Adams's father had been killed in a car accident. Kennedy tried to console his friend. "I wish I had your acceptance, your conviction. I wish I could believe that it's not over when you die, and that I would see my father again," Adams told Bobby. Adams never forgot the episode. Kennedy said to his friend he could find faith, even though Adams was not religious, and would find comfort in it.[12] He often invited Adams to go to mass with him. Adams saw Robert had an absolute faith in God and it made him oblivious to his lack of popularity at Milton. (Kennedy had arrived in Milton Academy two years after most of his classmates, so had a difficult time in catching up socially.) Kennedy wrote his mother he was,

> leading an underground movement to convert the school and am taking a lot of the boys to church on Sunday. Most of them like it very much, but I'm sorry to say I think the Protestant Ministers, who visit here are better speakers than the Priests at church."[13]

Bobby was considered a prig by his older brothers and sisters. Jack did not like his younger brother's puritanical attitudes and the

The Kennedys in 1948; from left: Jack, Patricia, Rose, Joe Sr.,
Jean, Bobby and Eunice with Teddy kneeling.
(John F. Kennedy Library and Museum)

Senator Robert F. Kennedy and family; from left: Ethel, Kathleen, Joseph, Robert Jr., David, Mary Courtney, Michael, Kerry and Christopher.

brothers argued over a wartime affair Jack had with a suspected Nazi sympathizer (the affair led to Jack's removal from Naval Intelligence and a new assignment to captain a small ship in the Pacific, PT-109). It has been said Robert was shocked at this behavior of his brother and at the marriage of his sister Kathleen, to a non-Catholic member of the British aristocracy, William John Robert Hartington, the eldest son of the Duke of Devonshire. Hartington and his family were devout Anglicans. How truly shocked Bobby was has to be questioned since he named his first daughter Kathleen and he worked and continued to stay by his brother's side through many campaigns, becoming his brother's closest personal advisor. Only a Catholicism more forgiving than judgmental of miscreants would have allowed Robert's course.

While in Harvard, Robert attended a Catholic seminar with a friend. A cleric spoke about non-Catholics, saying they all were headed for hell. Incensed, Robert openly disagreed with the speaker. The friend told Robert he should apologize to the man for the strong rebuke his classmate served up to the guest. Kennedy refused, believing that no Catholic should teach such a doctrine. A few years later, the Church agreed, and excommunicated the cleric for his teaching.[14] Later in life, when he had an audience with Pope Pius VI, Kennedy scolded him, saying the Church fell short of its obligations to blacks in South Africa and in America. He thought the Church should be in the forefront of the fight for social justice for blacks. Few Catholic layman would have been so bold with the head of their Church, but Robert Kennedy was a true believer of the Catholic faith and someone who could disagree with the men who controlled it. He was brought up to be devout in his beliefs and skeptical of the clerics of his church.

Everybody froze. A little boy had said something wrong, terribly wrong. Robert Kennedy had just walked into the room and the little boy was irrepressible as he ran up to the attorney general. It was at a Christmas party a *Washington Star* journalist had arranged for an orphanage, the first public event Kennedy had been to in weeks. The promise to attend came before the tragedy. He brought some toys.

Three weeks before Jack Kennedy had been killed in Dallas. "I had the feeling that it was physically painful, almost as if he were on the rack or that he had a toothache or that he had a heart attack," said John Seigenthaler about Robert's demeanor in those awful days after his brother's death. Kennedy, according to Seigenthaler, was "in a haze of pain."

The little boy from the orphanage ran up to Kennedy and said: "Your brother's dead! Your brother's dead!" With the sound of his own voice, the boy realized he had said something rash. All the adults stopped. The boy began to cry. Kennedy picked him up and held him.

"That's alright. I have another brother."

Many remember that bitter weekend in November 1963, its scenes have played over and over again from memory that can come as quickly as a video clip happened upon while clicking through television channels. Sometimes the shock returns in the oldest and dustiest stores: look up on the wall and away from everything else, a fading photograph of Jack Kennedy, or of Jack and Jackie together, reminds them. America grew old in an instant. All the tumult of the sixties seems to have sprung from that warm Friday afternoon in the minds of those who remember. While that may or may not be true, what is true is that the assassination changed everything for every American. If it changed everything for the country, what it did to Robert is nearly incalculable. Said Adam Walinsky, speechwriter and aide to Robert:

He's the only one of those people . . . associated with John F. Kennedy . . . that went on living after he died. The rest of them just stopped. They're relics. They go on functioning; they do things, but nothing's changed in them. Something got cut out and it stopped, as if somebody did a lobotomy on them. He was the only one that started a new process of growth.[15]

When Robert Kennedy finally went to bed, in the White House, in the early morning hours after November 23, he was heard to cry, "Why God?" That question haunted him in the weeks and months to come. He did not focus on the immediate causes of his brother's death. There exists but a handful of statements that voiced his thoughts about who killed President Kennedy. What Robert examined after the fatal shooting were questions of randomness or patterns, according to those who knew him best—whether we live through an arbitrary list of events or are guided by a universe of patterns and purpose.

He dismissed divine retribution as a cause. Somewhat mockingly, he told an interviewer that Lyndon Johnson liked to tell a story about a boyhood friend whose sled hit a tree and the boy became cross-eyed. "He said that was God's retribution for people who were bad. So you should be careful of cross-eyed people because God put his mark on them."[16]

Kennedy found his faith even as he opened books that posited existential answers to the mysteries of the universe. And from the accounts of those closest to him, there were many books. Books about the Greeks and about tragedies, and the works of Albert Camus predominated. Oddly, it was not Christian works that sustained him. Jackie Kennedy told Kennedy speechwriter Frank Mankiewicz after Robert's death: "The Catholic Church understands death. . . . We know death. . . . As a matter of fact, if it weren't for the children, we'd welcome it." It was Jackie Kennedy who gave Bobby a copy of Edith Hamilton's *The Greek Way* and they helped console each other through the months after Jack's death.

What Bobby sought was not a reason for Jack's death; he needed a way to continue living. "When the images of earth cling too tightly to memory, when the call of happiness becomes too insistent, it happens that melancholy rises in man's heart," wrote Camus in *The Myth of Sisyphus*. "This is the rock's victory, this is the rock itself. The boundless grief is too heavy to bear. These are our nights of Gethsemane. But crushing truths perish from being acknowledged."

Kennedy may have turned to the Greeks and other non-Catholic writers and philosophers, but through his journey in the corridors of doubt his faith never left him. It was in his first public speech after Jack's death, March 1964, that he used words from an old Irish ballad to express the grief that still clung to him and the country.

> Sheep without a Shepard;
> When the snow shuts out the sky –
> Oh, why did you leave us, Owen?
> Why did you die?

He was no longer questioning as a potential skeptic; the question came from pondering the deep mysteries of his own faith.

The crowds that attended his arrival to give the speech in Scranton, Pennsylvania were huge and Bobby Kennedy did not expect them. Two thousand people hindered his progress as he tried to leave the airplane and it took the police to clear a path through the people who crowded around wanting to touch him. Often in the months ahead, Kennedy dismissed the passions of the crowds as being for Jack. That may have been, but soon, they would be for "Bobby" too. He began to see that the need to carry on no longer involved himself alone; the religious man had a devotion to the earthly concerns of politics. In the aching hours after John Kennedy's death, Robert bore a solitary grief that even his enemies could notice and empathize with.

The eight-year reign of Dwight D. Eisenhower was coming to an end in 1960. A constitutional amendment that limited presidents to two terms probably chagrined Republicans who supported and saw the measure pass several years before the 1960 campaign. It passed in the wake of Franklin D. Roosevelt's four terms. Ike would have been their best candidate in 1960 and the likely winner had he been allowed to seek a third term. As it was, the race had no clear favorites and the Democrats were buoyed by the idea of regaining the White House. Jack Kennedy worked most of his political career to be recognized as a national figure. Since the surprisingly near miss in his attempt to become the 1956 Democratic vice presidential choice, he was constantly mentioned as a leading challenger to the Republicans in 1960. One issue loomed above the rest: his religion. As a Roman Catholic many non-Catholics believed his allegiance was divided and may very well default to the head of his church and not the Constitution.

The irony of the 1960 election is that Jack Kennedy held a measure of skepticism about his religion. His was more the conventional Catholic faith; Robert was the true believer. Yet it would be the elder brother who needed to defend himself and his church against an explosion of anti-Catholicism that the country had not seen since the failed campaign of Alfred E. Smith for president in 1928. Many thought a Roman Catholic remained unelectable. The Kennedys had a shrewder understanding.

Catholics and the way other Americans saw Catholics changed

in the 1960s. The changes came from within the Church as well as from economic and social conditions. The most important of the former was the election of Pope John XXIII and his two extremely influential encyclicals, *Mater et magistra* and *Pacem in teris* and the convocation of the Vatican Council. Among the social changes were decades of secular schooling of Catholics; it effected Catholics themselves and the people who grew up with and worked next to them, lessening their prejudice against Catholics. So, too, the economic mobility of Catholics moved them more into the American mainstream. JFK was a symbol and catalyst of change among Catholics.[17] Their numbers had doubled since 1928, to forty million. That most of them lived in important northern urban areas led the Kennedy camp to believe his religion would bolster his electoral vote count even as he lost some voters in other parts of the country, notably the South. They were right.

No American prejudice evaporated more quickly than that against Catholics. By the time Robert began his campaign, that another Roman Catholic, Eugene McCarthy, was also in the race drew little comment. Robert Kennedy could take a bolder stand because the climate was changing, within and outside the Catholic Church. He took stands favoring the relaxation of abortion laws and argued that the condemnation of birth control by the Vatican, especially in Latin America, had to be challenged. Murray Kempton, the veteran journalist, wrote that,

> There are persons so constituted that they can go nowhere without some piece of faith to serve for light. Robert Kennedy is a Catholic; and naturally he sought his faith there. It is the difference between his brother . . . and himself, the difference between those who are only properly orientated and those who are truly involved.

Kempton thought Robert entered into his fight against labor racketeers because he saw those men as having betrayed a "priesthood" and that Robert had become "a Catholic radical." Against the increasing cynicism of American politics, Robert represented "the survival of the spirit."[18]

We are a long way from the path Robert Kennedy trod. Even in that blistering year of 1968, America could still cling to shreds of hope. Hope got packed between the burning cities, the racial and class hatred. It had to be measured in moments because quickly frustrations and desperate measures spread to fill the emptiness. America did not lose its spiritual strength, it just could not cope with destructive urges that so long lay beneath the surface. Then, suddenly, with Robert Kennedy's murder, it was over. True believers in him packed up. Violent catharsis settled matters. America continued on a turbulent journey that may not yet have completely calmed.

Robert Kennedy did not cry out like a voice from the wilderness. He stood side-by-side with his generation of practical men who lead this country. The fraternal pragmatist would not let a romantic's instinct guide him. With his political antennae attuned to the advantage of his ambition, Kennedy knew exactly the odds of his presidential candidacy. Yet he was not a cynic. Deposited into those realist layers was a spirit so artfully assembled as to keep it from peeling away from its practical host. At this distance from the four decades of his life, it is futile to try. He may have been the last national politician who could use a true religious sense to steer his fellow citizens away from the deep wells of cynicism.

Senator John F. Kennedy with Ethel, Jackie and Robert
(© *Look* (Jones))

Attorney General Robert F. Kennedy with his brother
President John F. Kennedy in the Oval Office.
(© *Life*)

7

President One and a Half

. . . now create his equal, let it be like him as his own reflection,
his second self, stormy heart for stormy heart
—The Epic of Gilgamesh

THEY STARTED WITHOUT HIM. Robert Kennedy walked into a meeting already begun. He had been one hundred miles away, speaking to a convention of newspaper editors in Williamsburg, Virginia. "I don't think things are going as well as they should. Come back here," the president told his brother earlier that morning. The meeting Robert walked into on April 17, 1961 had been discussing the "invasion" of Cuba by anti-Castro exiles, men trained by the United States in Guatemala. They were on the beach, but stuck there, unable to move ahead or retreat. Eventually, over one thousand men would be sentenced to thirty years of hard labor by the Castro government. It was a major disaster for the country and the administration. The place they landed was called the Bay of Pigs.

Robert did not walk in cold. About a week before the CIA had briefed the attorney general. They told him that there was no chance the operation could end in total failure. Even if the invasion failed, the men could hide in the hills and become a guerrilla force. They found out later it was a fantasy force. In 1890 the area may have supported a guerrilla army. In 1961, it was a swamp. The twelve hundred armed men that attacked Cuba could not have been resupplied in that terrain. Nor were they told by their American trainers that the plan was for them to become guerrilla fighters if the invasion failed. Later, Robert Kennedy called the failed Bay of Pigs invasion the best thing that ever happened to the Kennedy administration because it learned early that advice from experts could be suspect—highly suspect.[1] President Kennedy from then on learned to question his experts more closely and in greater functional detail. Jack began to involve Robert in most of his administration's major issues after the Bay of Pigs. Robert became a proxy and an informant for the president, and sometimes the one to raise a trial balloon.

It also became a matter of organization. President Kennedy found that the government was larger and more diffuse than he expected; many agencies had overlapping responsibilities. No one person or group was in charge of bringing all the resources together. With a single person or task force gathering the information on any particular issue, the president could have one report summarizing expertise culled from all parts of the government. As Jack knew from his campaigns, Robert was a skillful organizer.

Finally, bringing Robert into more responsible positions within his administration Jack got someone with whom he could discuss decisions. Someone who could be trusted to be unfailingly loyal.

The Kennedy administration may have started without him in the role, but by the time of its unexpected and abrupt end, Robert Kennedy was the country's second most powerful man. "President One and a Half" as the people who wanted to emphasize the closeness of the Kennedys and the allotment of power during Jack's administration called him. Over the years that Jack served as congressman, senator and as campaigner for national office, no one with as much skill, ability and loyalty emerged as his brother Bobby. The reluctant attorney general seemed less reluctant to again put himself in service to his brother. This time, it was as much for matters of state as for family matters.

No president in the history of the country had such a close family member so powerfully imbued. After Jack Kennedy was dead, the Congress passed, and President Johnson signed, what became known as the Robert Kennedy bill, which forbade immediate family members of the president from being appointed to the cabinet. The combination of brother and cabinet member became a powerful one, and could have led, under more normal circumstances, to a long reign of Kennedys in the White House. The Kennedy bill passed with little debate.

Robert Kennedy's duties expanded to include foreign policy, national security issues; he had to keep watch over the CIA, be a diplomatic back-channel between the president and Soviet Union officials, oversee covert operations in Cuba and more, in addition to his cabinet post. The president largely bypassed the State Department, working nearly as his own secretary of state with many of its responsibilities going to an informal, non-official, group of national security advisors that included Jack Kennedy's most trusted people. It purposefully was separate and unaffiliated with the National Security Council. Jack Kennedy wanted to be able to analyze each crises before the more formal processes involving the State Department, the Joint Chiefs of Staff and the CIA. All these agencies, the Kennedys felt, failed Jack during the Cuban invasion.

"The National Security Council was worthless as far as dealing with any problems," said Robert. "I mean, you've go to make up your mind and then get the concurrence of the National Security Council. If you don't want [it] trying to decide, you have to decide before you go into a National Security Council [meeting]."[2]

By the time of the second Cuban crises in October of 1962, the Kennedys learned how to maneuver around its official councils and get the bureaucratic side of the military and security apparatus to conform to their wishes. The biggest mistake President Kennedy found out he made was the appointment of his brother. Jack Kennedy told Arthur Schlesinger while the invasion was still being fought on the Cuban beaches:

> I made a mistake in putting Bobby in the Justice Department. He is wasted there. Byron White could do that job perfectly well. Bobby should be in the CIA. . . . It's a hell of a way to learn things, but I have learned one thing from this business—that is, that we will have to deal with the CIA.

Because Robert Kennedy became a closer advisor to and strategic member of the Kennedy administration, his authority and confidence, and overconfidence, grew. It was another step in his development from that early, rigid young man to someone who could organize a presidency or bully a bureaucracy. And it raised his national stature.

Joe Sr.'s intransigent insistence on naming Robert to serve as the "president's lawyer," seemed a "clannish thing" to Jack at the time. Only after the Bay of Pigs did he, they, come to realize how truly shrewd, if unstated, their father's insight was. Jack Kennedy needed more than the campaign enforcer and loyal brother protector. He needed nothing less than an alter ego.

No modern ruler acts alone; even absolute rulers had courts, courtesans or even concubines that limited and enhanced their technically unconditional authority. Jack Kennedy would probably have found another way to act without the help of his brother. Luckily, he did have his brother on familial retainer making his burden easier. The fact that Robert was there, perched in the high councils of state along with experts and wise men, allowed Jack a freedom of action that might have been unavailable if his brother had not been available. Bobby could stand against the permanent government, the ones who are there before a new president arrives and remain after he leaves, with an alter ego that he could alternately use for appeals or denials, to show anger and to ferret out the details and issues generals, spies and other officials find awkward or unnecessary to tell the president.

Robert Kennedy wasted no time displaying his alter-ego status following the Bay of Pigs.

Ten days after being brought in to advise the president on the Cuban invasion, Robert Kennedy faced a National Security Council meeting where, Chester Bowles, undersecretary of state and originally favored by the administration, took the full blast of Robert/Jack's anger. Bowles, days before the meeting, told reporters he did not support the Cuban invasion, angering the Kennedys. At the meeting, he presented two State Department papers: one said Fidel Castro was securely in power and nothing less than a full-scale invasion of the island by the American military would dislodge the revolutionary leader. Robert Kennedy raged on for more than ten minutes upon hearing it.

The Jack Kennedy half of the paired egos sat quietly observing. As Bobby at other times and places, was observed to do, the president tapped his pencil against his teeth. No one doubted his brother was unloading the anger felt by Jack.[3]

President Kennedy's strategy was brilliant. It gave him the opportunity to both strongly express his anger and remain aloof from the process. Being chewed out by the boss could make the advisor gun-shy and less effective; the alter-ego president could be brought in and the relationship with the president would be much less strained.

Of course, if anyone took it on the chin, it was Robert Kennedy. Each time Jack/Robert's anger needed displaying, Robert's ruthless reputation grew.

Feat of Clay

In 1961 the Soviet Union began building the Berlin Wall. The move was not unexpected. East Berlin was hemorrhaging people, especially along the twenty-seven-mile border that divided the city. Early morning on August 13, the East Germans and Soviets began constructing a barbed wire "wall" to keep their citizens from fleeing to the West. Access to both areas of the city were normal, for West Berliners. East Berliners heading for West Berlin were being stopped at the last East Berlin train stations on the line and at the borders along the streets and sidewalks. President Kennedy knew The Wall was not built as a warning to the West but to corral its citizens. West Berliners saw it differently; they were not so sanguine about the limitations The Wall would put on their lives and for them such a barrier was no mere symbolism. The president would need to find a way to show his concern without being overly hostile to the Soviet Union.

That same evening a journalist and friend of Robert Kennedy, Marguerite Higgins, was vacationing on Cape Cod near the home of General Lucius D. Clay. He was known as the hero of Berlin especially to Berliners; he was commander of U.S. troops during the Berlin airlift in 1948 and strongly committed to keeping West Berlin out of the Soviet block. As Robert Kennedy noted in his diary during his 1948 visit to the city: "Clay is determined to stay in Berlin even if with only skeleton group." Higgins called Jim O'Donnell, a fierce partisan for Berlin, and suggested she could go down the street and ask her Chatham, Massachusetts neighbor Clay if he would be interested in being the administration's representative to Berlin. The appointment would be as special counsel to the president. It had no real authority; Clay would not command troops or create American policy on the ground in that newly-divided city. Even if unstated to Clay, Kennedy only needed to show Berliners that he was serious about protecting the West's portion of the city. Having a prominent Republican there also would be a way to ease the criticism of his domestic opponents.

Clay had been a chief fund-raiser for President Eisenhower and, at the time of 1961 Berlin crisis, served as president of the Continental Can Co. While Berlin had been one of his life's great causes, it was uncertain if the Republican backer and sixty-four-year-old retired four-star general would want to serve a forty-four-year-old, Democratic president. Higgins talked to Clay and he agreed to help. Higgins phoned her friend Robert Kennedy and he said he would make the recommendation to the president.

Clay had one caveat: never under any circumstances did he want to deal with Robert Kennedy. "I understand," said the president. He had laughed.

Problem is, the president never said this, at least in the source cited.

The presidential quote shows up in Richard Reeves' comprehensive book about the Kennedy administration, *Profile of Power*. Reeves cites page fourteen of Peter Wyden's *Wall: The Inside Story of Divided Berlin*. Go to the citation and one finds Clay telling O'Donnell of his reluctance to deal with Robert: "I'm a president's man, but I cannot abide that little brother of his." Higgins, told by O'Donnell of Clay's caveat, said she understood and that this particular presidential appointee would need to be managed by the president himself.

The incident has been used to demonstrate Robert's ruthless reputation and the president's knowing laugh so deliciously ends the interchange that the original source does not get checked. Evidently Reeves miscited the quote or simply made a mistake. As Wyden describes the scenario that led to Clay's appointment, Clay seems to be concerned more about dealing with the head man rather than his much younger appointee (Clay was nearly twice Robert's age at the time). A four-star general and chief executive of a large American corporation would not want to deal with younger brothers or underlings.

In addition, Clay's wanting direct contact with the president was crucial to the affect he would have in Berlin. He must have realized his presence was wanted as a symbol, that he would have no real authority. Military officers and ambassadorial officials already assigned there remained in charge. Clay wanted to push the Soviets using his own tactics and if seen as having direct authority of the president, he could get around his technically nonmilitary standing.

Robert Kennedy's abrupt, aggressive, intolerant and opinionated manner does not need a false tale to prop up an argument. Many people found him thus, friends as well as enemies. Dozens of first-source quotes are available. That Clay disliked the president's younger brother so may have been a temporary judgment since it is incongruent with later events.

Clay disliked Robert Kennedy so much that in late 1962, when the desperate attorney general needed $1.9 million on a moment's notice, to guarantee the return of Cuban prisoners captured during the Bay of Pigs crises, he signed a personal note for that amount. That is a lot of cash to help someone you cannot abide. Robert said that, "I was quite friendly with him personally and used to visit him frequently. When he had problems of this kind (having to get State Department approval for any actions he took in Berlin), he'd frequently come to see me." Clay went to see him to invite Kennedy and his wife Ethel to come to visit Berlin when they were planning their 1962 goodwill world tour.[4]

Nor would a relationship with an older, more conservative, military career man be out of character with Robert Kennedy. After the Bay of Pig crises, when the president appointed Maxwell D. Taylor to be his military representative and later his Chairman of the Joint Chiefs of Staffs, Robert became good friends with that older military man.

Abiding by misrepresented and non-events remains a hallmark of Kennedy critics.

"I'm a cattleman, Mr. Attorney General and these men look like animals who are going to die," said Alvaro Sanchez, a member of the Cuban Families Committee who Fidel Castro let visit the prisoners taken during the Bay of Pigs invasion. Sanchez told Kennedy in 1962 he could know this by seeing the back of their necks. "If you are going to rescue these men, this is the time because if you wait you will be liberating corpses."

"You can shoot them. Maybe you could have done that at one time, but you can't do it now. . . . If you want to get rid of them, if you're going to sell them, you've got to sell them to me. There's no world market for prisoners," James Donovan, who was sent to Cuba to negotiate for the release of the prisoners by Kennedy, told Castro.[5]

Robert Kennedy wanted to get the prisoners out of Cuba by Christmas. In the fall of that year, when Sanchez and Donovan visited Cuba, the situation looked hopeless. There had been discussion of paying ransom—although the administration did not call it that—for the Cuban invaders within a month after the invasion. Castro had first offered to release the prisoners for five hundred bulldozers. He specified the type of bulldozer: D-8 Super Caterpillars, which seemed better equipment to build missile and air bases rather than raising crops. Castro later amended the request to $28 million, what he estimated would be the cost of the bulldozers. The proposals went nowhere. The prisoners went on trial in March 1962 and were sentenced to thirty years of hard labor one month later. Bobby Kennedy then proposed to exchange the prisoners for $28 million worth of agricultural products, and did so without telling his brother. President One and a Half was beginning to take charge of events and he would be, by the end of the year, as fully charged in this endeavor as he had been against corrupt union leaders.

Once Donovan returned to the United States, and the Cuban missile crises was over, Robert turned his full attention toward the prisoners. Telling his Justice Department staff they were going to get the prisoners out of Cuba, at least one thought, at first, they were involved in planning a military invasion, not a negotiation.[6] "I really thought that with Bob Kennedy we were going do get something going with some boats and we were going down to get the prisoners out," said Louis F. Oberdorfer, an assistant attorney general. A negotiation it was and Castro was now expecting $53 million in food, drugs and machinery. American companies donated most of the necessary goods; they got in return assurances that the donations would be tax deductible. By December, it became a problem of transportation. The amount of goods necessary could not be solicited, prepared for shipment, transported to the common point of shipment to Cuba, then unloaded in Cuba all in less than two weeks that were left. Then Castro flung one, final hurdle at his American foes.

One half the one thousand, one hundred thirteen prisoners had boarded planes when the Cubans said the rest would board once an additional $2.9 million was received. Bob Kennedy called Cardinal Cushing of Boston, a Cuban Families Committee sponsor, to ask if he could raise the money quickly; time was running out, it was only a few days before Christmas. He raised $1 million from Cuban-American friends within a few hours. Then General Lucius Clay, also a committee member, signed a personal note guaranteeing the rest. The Cubans came home on Christmas Eve.

The operation was pure Kennedy: create a sense of urgency, add in an impossible deadline, put a diverse cross section of government into action by cutting through red tape and ignoring normal protocols, but mostly put a sustained, constant pressure on highly qualified people to press the limits of private and government systems and their own limits for a short-term, specific goal. He got the job done by quickly sizing up the situation, making a decision and plunging in head first. The process need not get bogged down in lengthy debate over what the situation called for: the way was clear and more discussion would only bring up obstacles. Once decided, checking and rechecking the final judgment only increases uncertainty; to do nothing is the worst sin. Delay in implementation merely makes the end that much longer off. Speed in action keeps everyone focused, keeping out doubt and fear. Bureaucrats need not apply. In this way, President One and a Half added another victory to the Kennedy legacy.

The curious part about the prisoner exchange is the personal responsibility Robert Kennedy felt. He had no real involvement in the planning and execution of the Bay of Pigs invasion, except for a postmortem he prepared with General Maxwell Taylor. It may have been a measure of how guilty his alter ego felt about the men dying in Cuban prisons. Jack told his aide Kenneth O'Donnell one morning, months after the invasion, that he could not sleep: "I was just thinking about those poor guys in prison down in Cuba. I'm willing to make any kind of deal with Castro to get them out of there." Cardinal Cushing noted when he talked to the president about the prisoners, "It was the first time I ever saw tears in his eyes."[7]

The president was fully committed politically, morally and personally to getting the prisoners out of Cuba. Yet the Cold War climate at the time blew so fiercely anti-Castro that any "bargain" with the dictator would have brought an unbearable amount of pressure on the administration by Republicans, members of Congress and even the military establishment. Many found paying ransom for the prisoners morally wrong. Some favored an out-and-out invasion of Cuba, as did ex-Vice President Richard Nixon when the president asked what he would do about Cuba. Nixon said he would find a legal excuse and "just go in."

Even when President Kennedy had a legitimate reason for

attacking Cuba, during the 1962 missile crises, when he could easily have had all the backing of his military and security advisors and members of Congress, he found an invasion of Cuba not only tactically wrong, but morally wrong, too. (It would be Bobby who would make the moral argument when Soviet missiles sought a Cuban launching pad.)

Because many others found bargaining for the lives of the Cuban prisoners wrong, the government could not directly pay Castro ransom. Instead, a patchwork of medical, farm supplies and other goods was assembled and shipped to Cuba. It all had to be donated by private business. Maybe someone else could have put the package together, but no one could bring to the project the authority Robert Kennedy did. Because he was the president's brother, his alter ego, Robert got things done a little faster, maybe received a bit more cooperation from the corporate community than someone without his stature would have.

The Cold War produced a large minefield of "bomb 'em" extremists, right-wingers aching for an invasion and even clandestine operations that actually did disrupt Cuban life and try to assassinate Castro. Despite Robert's wrong prediction, that there would be no long-term living with Castro, he and his brother set us on the road that allowed mutual accommodation that will probably last until Castro is dead.

Jack Kennedy may have been able to get the prisoners released without his alter-ego, but it was much easier to get the job done with President One and a Half.

When the Berlin Wall first went up in August of 1961, President Kennedy was so concerned he went sailing. What frightened the residents of West Berlin who had to live next to the brutal and authoritarian regime, brought almost a sense of relief to the Cold War president. He knew, and had been hinting for months, that such a solution would be good for East-West relations. East Berlin's citizens were leaving in droves, threatening the status quo. The Communist leaders could have selected a more dire solution than keeping its citizens home with a fence. (The Soviets and East Germans put up a barbed-wire fence first. They built the wall later.)

But it was over The Wall that American forces directly faced the Soviets two months later. Thirty American tanks on one side of The Wall pointed to an equal number of Soviet tanks on the other side. The world held its breath. President Kennedy did not seem to hold the same apprehension. His personal counsel to Berlin, General Lucius D. Clay, had been churning up trouble ever since he arrived in September. It looked as if the personal nightmare of President Kennedy would soon come true: some low-level official or member of the military could set off a chain of events that would lead to war. Everyone had a premonition of disaster except the president.

Jack Kennedy had something better, an ace in the hole: his brother and alter ego, Bobby.

The president felt secure about a back channel of communication he had with Soviet Premier Nikita Khrushchev that involved Robert and Georgi Bolshakov, a Soviet deputy chairman and its embassy's press attaché. Bolshakov was rumored to have direct contact to Khrushchev. He and Bobby became friends and the pair would meet regularly. Then Bobby would report the conversation to the president. Jack Kennedy used this connection to tell Khrushchev that if he would move his tanks away from The Wall within twenty-four hours, the American tanks would be removed thirty minutes later. On October 28, 1961, that is exactly what happened.

Robert Kennedy often served as unofficial yet most important go-between for his brother. The most important role as intermediary involved the Soviet Union. Yet Robert was also his broth-

Bobby and Jack at Jack and Jackie's wedding.
(John F. Kennedy Library and Museum)

er's representative to all levels of government, foreign officials and to the public. This ambassador-without-portfolio often was a surer, quicker way for the American leader to get his messages across with a kind of authority that no other elected or appointed member of government could achieve. When the situation demanded, Robert's "diplomacy" could be denied, as during the appointment of Lyndon B. Johnson as Jack Kennedy's running mate. A diplomat could be offended with such use. A brother might not feel so abused, especially a brother who well understood his president's goal and was absolutely sure that his brother would not use him in such a way unless he had a higher goal in mind. The Soviets understood the value of President One and a Half maybe better than some of the administration's own cabinet members who had to confront "that bony little face."

President Kennedy did that morning in 1962 what he might have done thousands of times over the years: give out PT-109 tie clasps and bracelets. Astronaut Walter Schirra, his wife Josephine and their children were the recipients as the president took the time to show the children his daughter Caroline's pony Macaroni. Schirra had recently returned from space, six orbits in the Sigma 7 Mercury space capsule. Had NASA been under the purview of the military maybe it would have been Schirra who photographed what other high-flying pilots did that month and whose pictures the president had just seen early on the morning of October 16. When he walked back into the Oval Office, he had his daughter in tow. What her father wanted to know first was if Caroline had eaten any candy. She did not tell him and ran off.

Turning from the weighty matters of his child's dental hygiene Jack Kennedy faced a roomful of America's most powerful men who had gathered to see and hear what the president heard hours before. American U-2 spy planes flying over Cuba had taken photographs of nuclear missile bases under construction. He had just returned from a campaign trip during which he had to refute charges made by a Republican senator that the Soviets had put nuclear weapons in Cuba. Apparently, the senator had no evidence since he never produced it. Evidence independent of those charges arrived before 9:00 a.m. that morning. The first thing he did was call Robert. "We have some big trouble. I want you over here."

Robert thought they looked like someone was clearing a field for a farm, Jack like a football field. They were indeed the construction site of nuclear missile bases and military analysts estimated they would be completed in ten days. Like nearly everyone else, Robert's first reaction called for a military strike. At first, he thought a pretext was needed like sinking "the *Maine* or something."[8] (No one else needed a pretext more than the existence of the nuclear weapons themselves.) As the gravity of the situation began to sink in, Robert scribbled something on a piece of paper and handed it to presidential counsel and speech writer Theodore Sorensen: "I now know how Tojo felt when he was planning Pearl Harbor."

Some officials thought the passing of the note inappropriate. The sentiment expressed did not strike the men as an accurate analogy. Yet the attack on Pearl Harbor shaped the lives of all these men, had become part, consciously or not, of every strategic military plan they discussed. Robert Kennedy would not win a prize for logic with he reference to Tojo, but for a course in ethics he might be given an A.

In the nearly universal call for military action among these generals, cabinet officers and presidential viziers Jack Kennedy foresaw the sure path to nuclear doom. If the first reaction to the missile sites by the advisors closest to him was to bomb Cuba, Jack Kennedy had no hope that a Congress or a country would follow a more limited, ultimately more rational approach to removing the offensive weapons. He had to get the military and cabinet publicly in favor of a blockade. Not that a blockade in itself would force the Soviets to remove the missiles, but the strategy would buy him time. The worst thing, the president knew, was to force the Soviets into a corner, from which they were certain to fight their way out. Kennedy needed to give his counterpart in Moscow some time to think and a blockade bought time.

The moral principle so instinctively, if not shrewdly, forced to the table by Robert Kennedy began a process that would lead to changing the minds of the men who that morning wanted a military attack. Only two ways existed to remove the missiles from Cuba: America would take them by force or the Soviets would be persuaded of their blunder and remove the missiles themselves. The military could not guarantee that they could remove all the missiles from Cuba, nor promise surgical strikes. Hundreds, perhaps thousands of civilians could be hurt or killed. The chances were pretty good that the Soviets would attack in kind, against American missiles in Turkey or by invading Berlin. Both scenarios would involve American and NATO reaction, and so the path to nuclear escalation lay open. Robert Kennedy's injection of a moral note to the technical and strategic discussions helped remind them that the true import of their decisions could not be determined in the week or two they had before the Soviet missiles would become operational—but by generations hence.

Time sobered heads inebriated by shock. Robert Kennedy began a process that took about six days. Most meetings the president did not attend. Security required that all seem normal at the White House. Pre-existing schedules were kept as much as possible. With Bobby present, Jack Kennedy could allow everyone to argue candidly with the hawkish members of the Executive Committee of the National Security Council, or Ex Comm, which was formed to decide on a strategy, thus keeping him noncommitted. During the Bay of Pigs discussions, the president found being present in early discussions prematurely bound him to a course of action. Robert pushed hard for the group to see the moral choice in deciding a course of action:

> [I] argued that, whatever the military and political arguments were for an attack in preference to a blockade, America's traditions and history would not permit such a course of action. Whatever the military reasons . . . in the last analysis [the hawks were] advocating a surprise attack by a very large nation against a very small one. This, I said, could not be undertaken by the U.S. if we were to maintain our moral position at home and around the globe. Our struggle against Communism throughout the world was far more than physical survival—it had as its essence our heritage and our ideals, and these we must not destroy.[9]

President Kennedy, said his aide Kenneth O'Donnell, believed his chances of making the wrong decision would have been much greater if he had been forced to make a quick decision. The president thought a quick attack against Cuba was wrong tactically. A blockade may have been a better decision morally, but that idea was left to his alter ego to argue. Bobby provided the moral argument giving the generals pause and Jack time.

Robert Kennedy's finest hours serving Jack's administration came when his actions coincided with his moral sense. Robert's worst moments came when he tried to match Jack's gamesmanship, as when he oversaw the covert actions aimed toward destabilizing Cuba and other countries not to his liking.

He never lost his combative nature; Robert Kennedy had been a rigid young man that experience softened but could not turn him into a diplomat. Yet with American and Soviet ships about to confront each other in the Caribbean, the president's brother took a message to the Soviet ambassador, Anatoly Dobrynin. They had met before, many times. Usually the discussions would turn into shouting matches. Dobrynin could not have been amused or comfortable facing the fierce anti-Communist, the rigid young man.

Two messages arrived from Premier Nikita Khrushchev; one evidently from the Soviet leader himself, its tone less belligerent and offered a way out of the Cuban missile crises without the intervention of military forces. The second message left much less room for negotiated settlement and could only lead, in the eyes of the men who were making the decisions, to war against Cuba or maybe a worldwide nuclear war. While committed to a blockade, the missile sites in Cuba would soon be completed and the military establishment wanted to take out the missiles soon. An American U-2 spy plane had been shot down (its pilot Major Rudolf Anderson Jr., the man who flew the original missions that spotted the Cuban missiles, died). Only days remained and President Kennedy was running out of excuses to give his generals.

Robert Kennedy suggested a reply to the first, less belligerent message, ignoring the second communiqué. President Kennedy dispatched his brother to discuss the American offer with Dobrynin.

During our meeting Robert Kennedy was very upset; in any case, I've never seen him like this before. True, about twice he tried to return to the topic of "deception," (that he talked about so persistently during our previous meeting), but he did so in passing and without any edge to it. He didn't try to get into fights on various subjects, as he usually does, and only persistently returned to one topic: time is of the essence and we shouldn't miss the chance.[10]

Dobrynin was a shrewd observer. Holding himself in check,

Bobby laid out a chance for agreement, that the American missiles in Turkey, officially under NATO control, would be removed after the Soviets removed their missiles from Cuba. Yet there was no doubt that Robert more than conveyed the terms of a proposal from his brother; his psychological disposition communicated the inner turmoil of his brother, too. A few days earlier Robert had been with Dobrynin in an opening discussion on the crisis. At that time, the Soviet ambassador noted that the "strange impression" Robert left seemed to be more a justification of the actions of his brother. They wanted to put the responsibility for anything that might result in confrontation over Cuba with the Soviets. He noted that the Kennedys did not seem entirely confident in the decision they made, to blockade Cuba.

They were not so confident. Jack Kennedy well knew the Soviets should not be given an ultimatum, although that is exactly the message he delivered, along with the quid pro quo of offering to remove missiles from Turkey. Yet the subtext of the message, the president's precarious position with his military and his own real fears of uncontrolled escalation of hostilities, could only be conveyed effectively by his brother. It was the role of alter ego and Bobby played it as well for the Soviets as he did for the American government.

Anyone could have carried a message offering a trade of missiles with the Soviets; the missiles in Turkey were obsolete and thus easily sacrificed. A telegram could have offered the trade. Robert Kennedy conveyed more: a human tone, a true sense of what his brother, and he, felt so that members of the administration, or foreign representatives for that matter, could be privy to something more than the position of the pieces on the president's game board. Since it was Bobby Kennedy, no one could go away without understanding that the president's position, that American interests, overlay a strong moral and spiritual foundation.

Attorney General Robert Kennedy conducts a staff meeting
of the Justice Department.
(© *Life* (Rickerby))

8

Justice For Some

Injustice is relatively easy to bear;
what stings is justice.

—*H.L. Mencken*

EVERYBODY OPPOSED IT, or so it seemed. Objections rose over his inexperience, his age, his propensity to seek results over paying attention to process; there would be charges of nepotism and Robert Kennedy himself did not want the job of attorney general of the United States. Joseph Kennedy Sr. remained adamant: Jack would need his brother in the cabinet if only to be assured one loyal person could be utterly trusted. Joe Sr. won out.

Robert Kennedy became the country's youngest attorney general since the days of Presidents Jefferson and Madison. What he lacked in years he more than made up in self-confidence. By all accounts the Kennedy administration assembled one of the country's finest array of legal minds. Robert's personal legal skills could not match much of the talent he assembled to work under him, but that is the point. He had enough self-assurance to hire the best and was not intimidated by his own youth and inexperience.

One of the most important people who objected to Robert Kennedy becoming attorney general was Bobby himself. He believed he would become involved in a wide range of controversial issues that could be difficult for the president. He also wanted to stop chasing "bad guys" as he had done the three years previous as senate counsel for the rackets committee. His father foresaw that unless Bobby became a member of the cabinet, as opposed to having an undefined role as counsel or advisor, his close relationship with Jack would make it difficult for other administration officials. A well-defined role like attorney general kept him close to his brother and allowed others to do their jobs with less real or perceived interference.

The question was how to make the announcement, which all understood could raise a controversy. "I'll open the front door . . . some morning about 2:00 a.m., look up and down the street, and, if there's no one there, I'll whisper, 'It's Bobby,' " Jack Kennedy told *Washington Post* reporter Benjamin Bradlee.[1]

President Kennedy did not need to hide his choice. He could not if he wanted to. The attorney general, for a number of reasons that included his unique relationship to his brother and Robert Kennedy's own nature kept him in the spotlight. Whether it was his supervision of the FBI and long-time Director J. Edgar Hoover (he became FBI director a year before Robert was born), organized crime or the civil rights movement, the confrontational nature of Robert Kennedy did not allow for a demur tenure.

The attorney general did not like the color, the brightness, of the young attorney's jacket. He liked the case that the Justice Department lawyer described to him even less. Kennedy asked the young man about his case, that of a post office tow truck removing another of its vehicles from a highway and receiving a ticket for it. Kennedy wanted to know who assigned the "traffic case" to him and the young man was reluctant to tell.

"You're going to tell me and you're going to tell me now,"

Kennedy demanded. The man finally did.

The post office truck should not get a ticket because it was a federal vehicle doing its duty. "You mean if I were driving on government business and went through some red lights at ninety miles per hour, I wouldn't get a ticket?" Kennedy wanted to know. Yes, the attorney replied. The attorney general was incredulous and said if that is true, it shouldn't be true. Later, when the subject of raises came up, every other man in that young attorney's group got one, except him. "I thought that little bastard had enough trouble with Cuba that he didn't have to bother with me," the man said after being asked about the incident.[2] Attorney General Kennedy bothered with issues great and small, but what still annoyed him more than anything else was poor preparation and disingenuous responses. He could pick on people, but not those he believed made a sincere effort to do their work.

It may not have been a physical reaction on Kennedy's part to J. Edgar Hoover, but Hoover certainly had a physical reaction to his new attorney general. Hoover arranged his office and personal appearance in a decorous, even fussy manner and expected the same of his FBI employees. Hoover always greeted visitors and staff meticulously dressed, never in less than a jacket and tie cinched to his neck. So when Hoover saw the rolled up sleeves and loosely slung "un-ties" of his newly-appointed boss, it must have angered him as much as the hot line Kennedy had installed so he could talk directly to Hoover by just picking up the receiver. Or Kennedy's direct manner, ignoring FBI policy and tradition, by going straight to the people Bobby wanted to talk to, not through the chain of command that ended with Hoover answering all attorney general queries himself. Hoover never had an attorney general walk into his office without an appointment or as little as a phone call, but Robert Kennedy did.

The FBI Director dealt directly with presidents, made friends with them to bypass his nominal boss, the attorney general, whose Justice Department controls the FBI. Hoover had to get used the fact that the president's brother would manage access to the president. Jack Kennedy met with Hoover every month or so to keep the peace; no one was fooled by the arrangement—Hoover nor the Kennedys. Each knew the opportunity for political collapse. So the uneasy, especially for Hoover, arrangement kept everyone functioning, but not satisfied. There is no doubt that Hoover despised Robert and distrusted all of the Kennedys.

"Goddamn the Kennedys," Clyde Tolson, Hoover's second in command and special companion, said to Hoover. "First there was Jack, now there's Bobby, and then Teddy. We'll have them on our necks until the year 2000." "I," said Tolson at another time, "hope someone shoots and kills the son of a bitch."[3]

Attorney General Kennedy never could bring Hoover completely under control. He did force the FBI to recognize the existence of organized crime, an area of law enforcement that Hoover did not want FBI involvement. Kennedy kept up his campaign against gangsters, crooked union officials and especially Jimmy Hoffa (the Justice Department had a "get Hoffa squad" assigned by Kennedy), but Hoover could and did thwart Kennedy's efforts to develop a central agency to collect all the information on organized crime developed by separate government agencies. After the assassination of Jack Kennedy, the emphasis on organized crime, such as it was, ended.

There were no black FBI agents when Kennedy became attorney general, no true agents. Two blacks were made agents during World War II to avoid the draft; they served as Hoover's chauffeur and office boy. Hoover acknowledged three more: all were drivers who did not conduct investigations. Kennedy managed to have only ten agents hired by the end of 1962. Hoover and Kennedy continued a mutual accommodation; neither enjoying the relationship. Hoover maintained his position in the end and little change was forced into his FBI. Only Hoover's removal or death could bring about the level of reform needed in the FBI.

Attorney General Kennedy succeeded in keeping the crafty FBI director at arm's length and brought about some recognition by the bureau of its responsibilities to investigate organized crime. There were even a few gains in the area of the bureau acting on behalf of protecting civil rights. Mainly, Kennedy failed to sway Hoover or his bureaucracy.

Relenting to the insistence of Hoover, Attorney General Kennedy approved the wiretapping of civil rights leader, the Reverend Martin Luther King Jr. One of King's associates, it was alleged, was a Communist. Hoover claimed it was Kennedy that urged the FBI to put wiretaps on King. While Robert resisted Hoover's requests for a time, having turned down one request in the summer of 1963, Robert finally agreed to a wiretap of King in the fall of the same year. He approved two separate wiretaps, for King's home phone and the phones of his offices at the Southern Christian Leadership Conference (SCLC). Both were to have been reviewed after thirty days, on November 20, 1963, Bobby's birthday, and two days before President Kennedy was assassinated. The FBI kept up the electronic surveillance until 1965.

The Kennedys believed nothing of consequence would be revealed by wiretapping King and that the evidence thus gathered would only exonerate him. Yet the attorney general did not review wiretapping authorization on King nor end it. Eventually, the electronic surveillance of King produced no important information. It did supply the country with personal information about King's sexual conduct and a glimpse of the kind of locker room talk the civil rights leaders used in private discussions but nothing to prove Communist affiliation or criminal wrong doing. Curiously, the King associate whom Hoover thought a Communist, and the Kennedys advised King to sever relations with, did not have his phone tapped by the FBI.[4] One would think that person's phone worthy of surveillance as much as King's and those of the SCLC.

Robert authorized the wiretapping under severe pressure from the FBI. There was political pressure, too, in the presence of an administration-supported civil rights bill in Congress. He did not want the taint of a Communist affiliation with King to appear in the press and threaten the bill. It was obvious the FBI campaign against King stood on purely political grounds.

King's own position on the wiretaps did not alter his support for the Kennedys. While he withheld support in 1960, King wrote he would have supported Jack's reelection in 1964. The SCLC had long supposed its phones were tapped and offices bugged and operated under the belief that their day-to-day business, their message of non-violence was not a secretive one.

The Kennedys were not leaders in the area of civil rights. Only when protesters risked life and limb as they sat-in, marched and bused themselves to call an end to Southern social practices and its segregationist laws did the Kennedys react. For example, a campaign promise to end segregation in federal housing "by a stroke of a pen" was not fulfilled right away. It took the clever protest of individuals sending, collectively, thousands of bottles of ink to the White House for the president to act.

Robert Kennedy's Justice Department barely kept up his end of the bargains made with campaign rhetoric. Since legislation took second place, behind litigation, in President Kennedy's administration, the early failure of the Department of Justice was felt bitterly throughout the civil rights movement. While black leaders noted that Jack Kennedy's did much more than previous administrations to help their cause; blacks as a whole just started to move faster than even white liberals thought possible to secure their own rights, certainly faster than southern states could handle without federal intervention.

Politics forced the Kennedys into awkward compromises that affected their standing with blacks, too. The most onerous executive actions, from the view of the civil rights movement, came in the appointment of federal judges in the South. Five of the lifetime appointments in the South, out of a total of twenty-five named, could fairly be described as hostile to civil rights, if not racist, segregationist and obstructionist. According to Victor S. Navasky, author of the most thorough examination of the Kennedy Justice Department:

> There can be no denying that during the turbulent Kennedy years these men, along with others whose records are spottier, consistently decided civil rights cases against Negroes (and white civil rights opponents) who had clear law on their side, as evidenced by the fact that their court rulings were invariably overturned in the upper courts.[5]

William Harold Cox is a prime example of the politically pressured selections the Kennedys made to appease friends and enemies among southern congressional members. Cox had been a college roommate of the chairman of the Senate Judiciary Committee, James O. Eastland (D-Mississippi). "[Eastland] could be standing right in the middle of the worst Mississippi flood ever known, and he'd say the niggers caused it, helped out by the Communists," said Lyndon Johnson.[6] Robert said that during his interview of Cox for the seat on the federal bench, Cox promised he would enforce the laws and the interpretation of the Constitution by the Supreme Court. He was convinced that Cox had been honest with him.

One of the first things Cox did was to rule against the 1960 Civil Rights Act and deny the Justice Department the right to inspect public voting records in Mississippi. Not one black person had, at the time, registered to vote in the county under dispute for over thirty years. No federal judged had been overruled more times on civil rights cases than Cox. He railed against the Justice Department cases brought before him in letters to officials and Justice Department lawyers. In 1964, Cox, in open court for a voting rights case, said blacks trying to expedite their registration in a Mississippi county were: "a bunch of niggers . . . acting like chimpanzees."[7]

Overall, the judicial appointments of the Kennedy administration were fair to good. It put ten black judges on the bench in the North, one of whom was Thurgood Marshall, who later would be named to the Supreme Court. The Kennedys were under no illusion that judicial appointments were above party politics. They actively sought the men among the party faithful; that politics intertwined with the appointment of justices came as naturally as appointing party chairmen or postmaster generals.

The attorney general's record within his own department is less subject to controversy. He assembled one of history's best legal teams and the quality of the litigation and other work from the Justice Department was superb. Most of the work done by the Justice Department is tedious, routine litigation, which Robert's department handled with a kind of enthusiasm that had not been seen in the Department of Justice for many years. The attorney general himself had rarely been seen by employees, until Kennedy came along. At first, attorneys and staffers alike were shocked when, in the midst of the daily toil, Bobby would walk in unannounced and ask them about their work. Without comparing the logs of them all it is hard to say if Robert traveled more than his predecessors, but it is undeniable that he visited many of the Department of Justice's offices scattered around the country throughout his term. His management style was to cheer on the troops in these inspections and remind his employees that their work was noticed and appreciated.

While the appointment of federal judges was troublesome, within the Department of Justice itself the civil rights picture was brighter. When Robert Kennedy began as attorney general, there were six lawyers in the department. He left with sixty black attorneys in place. His division of civil rights was among the department's busiest. The Kennedys thought most civil rights legislation would be futile; any bill that could pass the barrage of powerful Southern politicians would be so weak as to be useless. Their strategy was to concentrate on litigation, especially in the area of voting rights. If Southern towns and counties could be forced to follow the law and allow blacks to register to vote, then Southern politicians could not ignore the rights of blacks, went the Kennedy line of thinking.

Bobby Kennedy, age ten.
(John F. Kennedy Library and Museum)

9

Growing Up

With the ancient is wisdom;
and in length of days understanding.
—*Job 12:13*

WILLIAM O. DOUGLAS SAID YES when Joseph P. Kennedy, Sr. asked if he would take Bobby along when the Supreme Court Justice visited Soviet Central Asia. The Soviets said no in 1951 when Douglas and young Kennedy first applied for travel visas. Joseph Stalin was still ruling the USSR and Douglas had been identified as an American spy. The pair continued to apply and the Soviets continued to deny them visas each year until 1955. Although his wife Mercedes could not fathom why Douglas would want to drag along "that rigid young man," the trip proved Joe Sr. sometimes knew his sons better than they knew themselves.

Douglas simply wanted to see the effects of Soviet communism on Central Asia. He liked traveling to remote spots and was an unreconstructed mountain climber and hiker. Few Americans had been to the region nor had many Europeans traveled to that large territory with its diverse assortment of countries, languages and religions. Kennedy went along reluctantly. His father knew that his socially awkward, politically inflexible son could use a dose of realism. Communism as he encountered it through the McCarthy committee was nebulous compared to the daily reality that system wrought in countries whose histories included only monarchies and dictatorships. Like his brother John, who attended the London School of Economics and Political Science to study under the Marxist political scientist Harold J. Laski, Joe Sr. wanted his third son to understand firsthand the political issues of his times. Since John was more the intellectual, his father sent him to study in the famous school for the social sciences. Robert, never the studious type, would be better served by firsthand experience.

It was from such direct encounters that Robert Kennedy learned best. Throughout his life he found understanding from direct contact with people and places rather than from the books he avoided as a youngster. The 1955 trip with Douglas may have had as much effect on Kennedy as any other event in his life except for his brother's death. Kennedy encountered people whom he knew only as caricatures. On the first leg of his trip, aboard the ship that took Kennedy and Douglas from Teheran to Baku, he spotted a woman tucking in one of the crew members. "Captain and crew insisted the woman was a doctor not [a] nurse," wrote a surprised Kennedy. He would encounter many women whose roles did not fit the American idea of female careers while in the Soviet Union and even was administered to by a woman doctor when he got sick on the trip.

Since America and its allies began their involvement in the Cold War, Americans were fed a steady cultural diet of godless, soulless Communists whose sole aim was world domination. It may have been the first time he understood that the people who found themselves under the thumb of the Soviet rulers were only trying to achieve as best they could the same aims as the people in the communities of America. The pair toured farms and factories, witnessed court proceedings and entered churches, many churches. All the while Kennedy took notes, recording a farm's annual output here, the salary of a truck driver there. He noted dancers in Baku were paid one thousand rubles a month, the same as a streetcar driver, and that rent was fifty rubles a month for three rooms. Whenever he entered a store, Kennedy noted the cost of things (especially postcards, which he often found hard to obtain). He was arrested for taking pictures and lifted many toasts "to the friendship of the young people of Russia and the USA" but wrote mostly unemotional remarks. He self-consciously played the role of American youth representative, portraying a boy scout's pluck to the unlucky subjects of oppression.

> I fell off my seat in the jeep going over a bump. We got stuck in a stream and water came into the back of the car. After I fell off, the two of the three Russians, who were riding with me, grabbed hold me for every bump afterwards. It did not speak very well for the strength and resilience of American youth.

At the beginning, Douglas had to admonish his young friend not to be so combative in his approach to meeting and questioning people. A foreign service officer was assigned to travel with the pair, Frederick W. Flott. While Flott awaited a Soviet visa, Douglas and Kennedy forged ahead. Flott got his visa, and eventually caught up, but not before hearing what became a repetitive story: "We liked Justice Douglas. We can see he is a wise man. But [great sigh, looking at the ground] with him there is a Mr. Kennedy. He seems always to be saying bad things about our country."[1] A Soviet tourist guide had given the trio a footlocker full of Russian caviar, which the unfortunate Douglas could not eat. Kennedy thought all Russian food dirty and would not eat it. So it was up to Flott to limit himself to a ration of three jars of caviar every meal. When Ethel met her husband at the end of the trip, she was shocked at his shrunken appearance. "What have you done to my husband?" Part of it came from an illness Kennedy suffered and part because he would eat and drink very little due to an irrational fear of "Communist food."

Kennedy relented and began to notice a dual ignorance between the Cold War enemies. "People have no idea how our system of government works. We, I think, are equally ignorant of their system." The struggle between the Soviet system and the United States government depended more on economic defeat, noted Kennedy in the aftermath of his trip, and he became more sympathetic to the plight of the people living under Communist rule. "If we are going to win the present conflict with the Soviet Union, we can no longer support the exploitation of native people by Western nations. We supported the French in Indochina far too long."

Whatever changes Kennedy experienced became more evident as he began to survey the landscape of American poverty and prejudice and how it compared to the Soviet Union. In the ghettos and in the communities of the sharecroppers, in the mines and factories of America, Kennedy saw portents of disaster far more treacherous than a Soviet missile.

Andy Williams, the singer, was among the visitors to Hickory Hill, Robert and Ethel Kennedy's home in the horse country of McLean, Virginia. Any regular visitor to the Kennedy home had to get used to the uncanny atmosphere, with its fraternity-like rowdiness and lots of athletic activity. Williams thought he at least could be spared the Hickory Hill acrobatics since he had a broken toe. He might have been allowed had there been another person to round out a doubles tennis match. "Don't look for sympathy from us," Ethel Kennedy told Williams as she drafted him. His fellow tennis players included mountain climber James Whittaker, whose legs were still in bandages from an operation on his veins and Ted Kennedy, in a heavy metal brace he still needed to wear because of the broken back he suffered a year before in a plane crash. Ethel herself was not wounded, but she was pregnant, in her last trimester.[2] What else could Williams do?

In Robert, Jack Kennedy found his doppelgänger; in Ethel Skakel, Robert found his. She moved as quickly as he, competed with the same ferocious energy. Sports dominated their early lives. If not more so, Ethel practiced her Roman Catholic faith as closely as Robert. Both shared an aversion to off-color jokes and a priggish attitude toward sex. One Washington hostess would arrange seating by passing out, instead of table cards, nuts and bolts, for women and men respectively, and the guests would have to find their match. Not when Ethel and Bobby were guests; plain table cards were just fine then.[3] Yet far from being prim and proper, Ethel had a kind of wild, fun streak that showed itself time and time again. Their Hickory Hill parties became famous for their pranks and games, infamous for the guests being tossed into the pool.

Ethel also had a habit of tossing drinks into the faces of people she thought a bit too proper or if the conversation was not to her liking. People had bowls of salad upturned over their heads, too. Screeching children seemed everywhere, plus pets (ducks, geese, horses, ponies, lizards, iguana, turtles, rare bird species, cats and even a sea lion as well as Bobby's not so well-regarded dog Brumus) running amok on expensive carpets and sometimes sinking their teeth into or peeing on innocent guests or biting Ethel, as a pet coatimundi did once. Ethel once greased a pig and set it loose in the dining room. Government officials would be taking important phone calls as party guests rush passed them playing hide-and-seek games. Special guests called for special games, as when Robert Frost came for dinner. All the guests were given pens and pads and asked to write a poem including the poet laureate. Once Ethel placed live bullfrogs as centerpieces for a Saint Patrick's Day

Did You Hear the One About . . . ?

How do you quickly find Milton Berle? That was the dilemma as Kennedy told his staff that the speech he would be giving in upstate New York was too serious. Berle, who he had seen that week, "wouldn't mind" helping out with a few jokes, Kennedy said. Unable to find the popular comedian's phone number, his staffers made up their own jokes for the speech. "God, is he slipping!" exclaimed Kennedy as he read the faux Berle. "I mean they are really bad. He is really losing his touch. Isn't that too bad."[4]

Too bad for Kennedy. Humor was necessary to soften his harsh, ruthless, image. Joke and speech writers worked overtime to add some of Jack's sparkle to Bobby's not particularly bright speaking style. "I want to assure you I have no presidential aspirations," Bobby told the Women's National Press Club in 1965, "nor does my wife, Ethel Bird." President Johnson's wife was affectionately known as Lady Bird.

That was one more family characteristic Robert had to compete with: the famous Jack Kennedy wit. Bobby did not turn himself into a widely admired orator, but he eventually was able to speak comfortably and coherently. Humor peppered his public remarks as he become more comfortable at the dais. He could deliver the punch lines written by speech writers and professional comics as well as any politician, but no better than most. Robert was no Jack Kennedy.

There was the humor that spoke to Bobby's Roman Catholic beliefs: upon hearing Soviet Premier Nikita Khrushchev report his Cosmonauts had not seen any signs of God while they were in space, Kennedy said: "We can only suggest that they aim—with the rest of mankind—a little higher." After a visit with the Pope, Kennedy could not help but tweak the reporters who, through most of his public life, followed his every movement: "We had a friendly audience with Pope John. . . . He blessed us all, including the American newspapermen who were traveling with us, most of whom were not Catholics. He assured them that it was just a little blessing and wouldn't do them any harm."

Reporters get bored listening day after day to the same stump speech candidates are forced to give, and so do the candidates. Kennedy's signature quote came from George Bernard Shaw, "Some people see things and say, 'Why?' But I dream things that never were, and say, 'Why not?'" The press corps knew this meant the speech was over and used it as a signal to return to their buses. Once, Kennedy changed the last line to "I say, 'Run for the bus.'" His daughter Kerry once rushed up and threw her arms around him and gave him a kiss: "Please Kerry," he told her, "I told you—only when there are cameramen present."

The humor could be dark, too.

During a wake for his brother-in-law and a friend who died in a plane crash in 1966 Kennedy said: "Hackett [a friend of Kennedy since prep school] and I have so much experience at this thing that we're offering a regular service for funerals. . . . We pick out a cheap casket to save the widow money. You know they always cheat you on the casket. We pick passages from the Bible and do all we can to ensure an interesting and inexpensive funeral."[5] On a plane over Iowa, with lightening flashing all around threatening to hit the small chartered aircraft, Kennedy stood up in the middle of the cabin and shouted to the half a dozen reporters, "Don't worry, men. You're safe as long as I'm here." They laughed and he returned to his seat and turned to another reporter and said "And you know the kind of luck my family has had with these things."[6]

Occasionally, the humor fell flat. In an extremely tense, life-threatening situation, as the Reverend Martin Luther King Jr. and other civil rights protesters were trapped inside a church, with riotous gangs outside waiting to beat, or kill the frightened group inside, King was desperately trying to get the aid of Attorney General Robert Kennedy. Army troops had been sent, but were taking a nerve-rackingly long time to arrive. Wanting to defuse the situation, Robert, on the phone, told King "As long as you're in a church, Reverend King, and our men are down there, you might as well say a prayer for us." King did not appreciate the joke.[7] Others in similarly tense confrontations during the civil rights protests took a warmer view of his gallows humor. Edwin O. Guthman, on the scene as James H. Meredith was being enrolled as the University of Mississippi's first black student, told Robert that the situation was deteriorating. "It's getting like the Alamo," he told the attorney general. "Well, you know what happened to those guys, don't you?" was Bobby's reply.

Kennedy could easily joke about his image and his political standing. A South Carolina politician admitted to Robert in a letter that although he was not politically sympathetic with Kennedy, he still hung a photo of him in his office. Kennedy, realizing what many Southern whites thought of him, wrote in his invitation to the man to visit, "We eat little children on Tuesdays but almost any other day would be fine."[8]

He could also be impish. At a luncheon held by the ambassador in Venezuela, Bobby was found by *The New York Times* reporter in the pool. He invited Martin Arnold into the water. Arnold did not have a suit. Bobby said he was in the pool without a suit. Arnold figured if *he* was in there without a suit . . . so he peeled off his clothes and dove in. As the people gathered for the reception, Kennedy left the pool, wearing a bathing suit. Arnold noted the ambassador was very upset.[9]

dinner table.[10] It was a "madhouse" by many accounts, including one by Robert Jr., who asked for permission to attend boarding school to get away from the rowdy atmosphere.[11]

"Scatterbrained" was the polite term for the unscholarly, unworldly Ethel Skakel. Once, when speaking with a Native American woman, Ethel asked if she lived in a teepee. She also wondered aloud to a Supreme Court justice why he objected to prayer in school "since God is everywhere," to a Japanese government official if it is true his country's cats have no tails and why she could not go to Egypt to see the pyramids (her husband was senator from New York with the country's largest Jewish constituency and Egypt was Israel's enemy at the time). Was Truman Capote, you know, a homosexual, Ethel wondered aloud to a bemused Jackie Kennedy.[12]

Ethel's family, the Skakels, were rich, like the Kennedys, full of sports and fun, like the Kennedys, but unlike their in-laws, not interested in politics. Catholic schools tried to educate Ethel, who paid more attention to her horse riding skills (a nationally recognized rider when she was young). It was in Manhattanville College of the Sacred Heart that Ethel met Bobby's sister Jean, through whom the future couple met, skiing in Canada. Bobby's interest, at first, was for Ethel's sister, who eventually married an architect and moved to Ireland. It took four years before the two began to seriously date.

Like with most young men, marriage brought changes to Bobby Kennedy. He dressed more attentively. He outdid his siblings in the competition for family, being the first to father a child in the next generation of Kennedys, the first of Joe Sr.'s grandchildren. They had eleven children in all, seven in the first eight years of marriage, four in the last years (including one after his death). Twice during television appearances in 1964 he failed to list his children by order of birth.

I took a vote among my family to see their preference for president. Three are for me, two are for McCarthy, two are leaning for Humphrey, two are undecided and the youngest is sticking with Dr. Spock.[13]

Jackie Kennedy brought an élan to the White House and the administration—haute cuisine, Pablo Casals, Igor Stravinsky, George Balanchine and hung Cézanne on its walls. She was its unofficial minister of culture.[14] While Ethel had a wardrobe of the world's finest couture—roast beef and mash potatoes were more often the fare at Hickory Hill. André Malraux, the French novelist and Minister of Culture was honored at the White House and Leonard Rose, the world-famous cellist, played in his honor. Malraux visited Hickory Hill, too. Exposed to the menagerie, the romping children and adults, he spoke, in English as he rarely did, "This house is 'hellzapopping.'"[15]

Not that the McLean, Virginia house was just fun and riot. Arthur Schlesinger organized a series of lectures for Bobby and Ethel and for members of Jack's administration to attend. He garnered people from Isaiah Berlin to Al Capp and John Kenneth Galbraith to lecture. Alice Roosevelt Longworth, who was part of Washington's social and political scene for sixty years said, "They sounded rather precious, but there was nothing precious about these lectures. It was all sorts of fun."[16]

Bobby's shyness as an adolescent seemed to have remained with him throughout his life. He was always awkward at small talk, did not socialize well at dances, often refusing to go, and was a bad dancer according to his mother and sisters. Ethel helped change this. She helped draw out her husband, starting stories then encouraging her husband to finish the tale. Hickory Hill's boisterous nature came from Ethel. Where

Bobby sometimes seemed abashed at his presence among the New Frontiersmen, Ethel reacted by poking the powerful in the ribs; she once greeted a visiting foreign official not with a handshake, but a blast from a can of shaving cream she brought from behind her back.

Ethel brought Bobby another step closer to a fuller image of himself. The workaholic, stifled altar boy became a center of fun and interest during the Hickory Hill years. You could put on the Ritz in the formal gatherings at the White House, but you should have been prepared to soak those tuxes and evening gowns in fraternal pool water when you visited Bobby and Ethel. It was a ritualized hazing, the famous "boat treatments," a kind of baptism that marked your acceptance into the sect of power. A push into the pool and the chlorine-christened reemerged part of the happy few, their conditions gentled, their loyalties affirmed. Scatterbrained as many described her, Ethel Kennedy knew how far to push people and taught her husband the joys of power.

President Kennedy ordered an end to the Hickory Hill dunkings after one too many visiting foreign government official was aqueously initiated.

Another initiation Robert Kennedy received arrived through a blistering barrage of bitterness and rage. He admittedly was hardly aware of black people, "Negroes" in the vernacular of his times. The dinner table talk of his youth rarely strayed into the violence second-class citizenship bestowed on blacks, particularly in the South with codified rules of race separation. Northern states had their own peculiar methods of keeping whites and blacks apart that worked quite well (and still does). Separate was not, is not equal, but brutally vicious in its allocations of wealth and authority.

The young law student did involve himself in challenging the segregation policies of the University of Virginia. When taking responsibility for inviting lecturers for the university's Student Legal Forum, he asked and got an assent from Ralph J. Bunche, a diplomat who would go on to become a United Nations General Secretary, and was black. The trouble was the school's policy did not allow the seating of blacks and whites together, a stipulation required by Bunche. The school acquiesced after a vigorous protestations by Bobby. It was his first civil rights battle. He had a long way to go since at the time Robert and Ethel were also members of country clubs and other organizations that restricted membership to whites.

From the beginning of Jack Kennedy's administration, he and his brother worked hard on civil rights. Much of the time, the issues came to them, as when blacks decided they should attend the same colleges and universities as whites or when the Freedom Riders wanted nothing less than desegregated travel so blacks could use the same buses and bus terminals allowed whites. There was as much fear that white racists would, as indeed they did, riot, beating up civil rights protesters, the occasional reporter and government official. They did not want disorder to reduce the slim margin by which Jack entered the White House. They also initiated some civil rights actions. Immediately, both Kennedys used their executive authority to push for the desegregation of the Coast Guard, somewhat of a public relations move, and the Department of Justice, changes that had some lasting effect.

Blacks demanded much more. Robert Kennedy tried to balance the speed of change, not wanting to push Southern whites too hard nor appear to be stifling the pace of change. He thought he was doing a pretty good job of it, trying hard to keep the peace while getting blacks more and more equal access to public facilities and institutions. He pleaded with civil rights leaders to push more strongly for voting rights, since his political mind saw that a strong voting block could not be ignored by Southern politicians if they wished to remain in office. Then came a meeting he asked to be arranged between himself and leaders of the black community, artists, writers, actors and activists. It took place in a Kennedy family apartment on May 24, 1963. Said Kenneth Clark, author, educator and psychologist and a leading figure of the black civil rights movement:

> The most intense, traumatic meeting in which I've ever taken part . . . the most unrestrained interchange among adults, head-to-head, no holds barred . . . *the* most dramatic experience I have ever had.

It shook Robert Kennedy to the core of his beliefs. Many people in the room agreed with him, believed with him that the Kennedy administration had done more for civil rights than any administration since the Civil War. But that was said. What was also said, what was shouted, verbal punches again and again at the increasingly angry, red-faced attorney general was the uselessness of white good intentions and the boiling fury of blacks who no longer could believe in law or country. The attack on Kennedy was led by Jerome Smith, a civil rights worker who some had estimated spent more time in jail, had been beaten up more times than any other CORE (Congress of Racial Equality) member. James Baldwin, the novelist, arranged the meeting with Kennedy and leaders of the black community. Kennedy's idea of the meeting was one to discuss policy, what government could do, how laws and regulations could change the status of blacks in America. The meeting became a horrible, verbal beating and Bobby the punching bag.

Lena Horne, the singer, was among the people who attended the meeting:

Ethel and Bobby on their wedding day.
(© Stettner)

This boy [Smith] just put it like it was. He communicated the plain, basic suffering of being a Negro. The primeval memory of everyone in the room went to work after that. . . . He took us back to the common dirt of our existence and rubbed our noses in it. . . . You could not encompass his anger, his fury, in a set of statistics . . .

As Smith stammered his angry barbs at Kennedy, Kennedy turned away from him. That turned the rest of the meeting's attendees away from Kennedy. Smith claimed his patience nearly gone, and would use violence if plain justice did not respond to peaceful protest. "Never! Never! Never!" was his response when asked if he would fight for his country. The super patriot in Bobby became horrified. Others told him that if he was the best white America could offer and he was insensitive to the anger displayed in that meeting, nothing but giving blacks guns would satisfy them, that blacks would have to kill white people in the streets.

"Bobby became more silent and tense, and he sat immobile in the chair," said Clark. "He no longer continued to defend himself. He just sat, and you could see the tension and the pressure building in him."

After the meeting, some of the people who had sat silent later told Kennedy they were sorry he had to go through the assault, that they understood how hard he and the president had worked to help blacks. They could not, however, say that at the meeting: their standing in the black community would have diminished and their effectiveness as leaders waned.

It was the most important lesson any American public official had ever received on the anger and frustrations underlying segregation, poverty and the entire black experience. Most other prominent men might have walked out of the room quickly.

Robert Kennedy stayed there until the meeting fizzled out three hours after it began. He was angry, hurt and disgusted with the entire process. His reaction could have been that the entire issue was futile and a waste of time.[17] Something very different happened. Bobby changed.

There are many who believe the recognition of death changed Robert Kennedy. In the weeks after his brother's murder his spiritual search for meaning made him into the more sensitive, less brittle man than the one he displayed tracking gangsters, running campaigns and helping his brother rule. Of course it must be true Jack's murder changed him; few of us could survive such trauma without affect. Yet if one looks carefully, the change undergone by Kennedy came from every part of his political life. Slowly at first, then more quickly as he ruled in its corridors, Robert learned of power's ultimate futility when unaccompanied by compassion. We might be uncomfortable with the language—cynical as we are today after years of being trained to see the worst of every public official, expecting every president to slip into folly—but the only words capable of describing what Kennedy saw in his journey revolve around love.

America's institutions had failed. What should have been the purpose of schools, churches and families got lost. The love and support necessary to develop whole, fully alive, contributing members of America's communities shrunk in the face of the new superpower's disregard for some basic human needs. Hundreds of thousands of people were slaughtered since World War II for questionable Cold War tactical gains, and millions more faced destruction if rational behavior failed to release nuclear weaponry. America's technical achievements failed to bring along vast numbers of people whose inclusion should be essential to the republic's success. That is not what they understood. The people our institutions failed clearly understood America found them unnecessary, that they need not now nor ever apply.

Kennedy's education in the lands of Central Asia showed him that people under the most dreadful political conditions can be infinitely resourceful. A decade later, as he began traveling to places as far away from his own experience culturally and economically as was the Soviet Union geographically and politically, came a more dreadful understanding of how easily the human soul could be thwarted. He saw that only through a cooperative effort among the members of a community could individuals protect themselves from the destructive potential of the modern state. If hope would appear, first people would need a way to bring that hope into themselves, to believe in their own creative and spiritual potential.

His own personal awkwardness as a young man, the shyness and feelings of intellectual inferiority helped him see more clearly than others how awfully simple it is to wound the soul. "He's got this humility because he knows he's not clever—in a group of sophisticated intellectuals he has very little to say, but he believes that he can contribute something to trying to stop what is evil."[18]

A curious thing happened in 1968 as Robert Kennedy prepared to campaign in Oakland, California. He had scheduled a meeting in Oakland's black section. Kennedy asked if any good would come out of the meeting. His campaign aide John Seigenthaler replied "it will be alright." Robert had his own prediction: "No. It's going to be a very disorganized meeting . . . and there's going to be some anger." Seigenthaler remembered:

> He was quite right. It was a rough, gut-cutting meeting in which a handful of people stood up and blistered white society and him as a symbol of white society. He sat there and listened and took it, and answered their questions directly

and bluntly. He didn't pull any punches with them.[19]

Seigenthaler apologized to Kennedy for putting him through the ordeal. Kennedy had been there before and took away from earlier experiences an understanding even those closest to him did not know at the time.

I'm glad I went. . . . They need to know somebody who'll listen. After all the abuse the blacks have taken though the centuries, whites are just going to have to let them get some of these feelings out if we are ever going to settle down to a decent relationship.[20]

They returned to Oakland the next day. Word of the meeting had gotten around the community and local people had been told to treat the candidate with respect. Members of the Black Panthers were told to shush as Bobby began to speak. The crowds were so thick Kennedy's car was stuck and could not get out after his speech had ended. Remarkably, some of the very community people who had been so boldly callous the night before got out in front of the car, and the Black Panthers, too, helped to clear people from the car so the candidate could keep his schedule.

Educating Robert Kennedy, sometimes forcing him into growing up, meant putting him in direct contact with people, places and events. Reams of reports and volumes of books could not do for him what one handshake in the barrios of Brazil could teach. Kennedy's personal confidence grew with marriage and children, as do the lives of most people. Growth was a constant theme in his life, a steady evolution and not based on irregular, epiphanic interruptions.

The more direct contact with people he came into, the more Robert Kennedy grew. It was not a guise for opportunism. He was not a chameleon using change simply to feed his personal ambitions. No human being is fully-formed at birth and nearly everyone changes, matures. More under suspicion would be the dogmatic politician whose response to changing conditions falls on rigid ideas solidified early in a public career.

Finally, Robert Kennedy grew up politically in an era of change nearly unmatched in American history. Within one generation from World War II and Vietnam was a difference so vast it would be difficult to imagine anyone but the most serious ideologues immune to it. Change did not occur in a healthy way. Violence, disaffection, hate and fear, whose echoes are only now beginning to fade, accompanied America's journey. Bobby Kennedy intended to lead in his era of turbulence by action and example. Future politicians could lead with no less conviction and hope.

10

Moral Pragmatism

There ought to be patriotic citizens ready to plunge into the stream
and save the boat from drifting towards the rapids.

—*James Bryce*

FOR TWENTY MINUTES the Democratic National Convention
watched a documentary on the life of Robert F. Kennedy. Then
it nominated William Jefferson Clinton to be its nominee to run
for president of the United States in 1992. The election of
Clinton ended the rule of politicians taken from the pool of
young men who served in World War II, Jack Kennedy's generation. What echoed in their hearts and minds, Pearl Harbor, the
Great Depression, the rise of fascism and communism, was half
a century old when the Vietnam generation, Bill Clinton's era,
took over. Robert Kennedy, although contemporaneous with
Ronald Reagan, George Bush and Richard Nixon, seemed more
a part of the politicians who claimed the era of civil rights and
war protests as his political coming of age.

It only seemed that way. Bobby was a Cold Warrior spouting
as much vitriol against the "evil empire" as had Reagan. The difference is that Kennedy could encompass change, grow in the
same ways that other politicians harden their beliefs. It opened him
to charges of pandering, discrediting his genuineness. The legend
of the good Bobby and the bad Bobby posed a divided man.

Robert and Ethel Kennedy greeting Lyndon B. Johnson.
(© White House (Stoughton))

Robert Kennedy took himself out of the race for president on January 30, 1968 and he would stay out of the race for any "foreseeable" circumstance. He originally would have told the National Press Club breakfast he would stay out of the race for any "conceivable" circumstance, but Frank Mankiewicz, his speech writer, persuaded him to change the wording to remove the tone of absolute finality. Even as he spoke, the North Vietnamese provided an unforeseeable event.

Seventy thousand Communist soldiers launched an offensive that same day [a shocked America would not find out until the next day]. No one expected the Communists to attack during the lunar New Year celebration 'Tet. From the demilitarized zone that separated North from South Vietnam to Camau, well to the south of Saigon, Communist soldiers were able to infiltrate the urban areas of South Vietnam, the huge American military complex at Camranh Bay and, most startlingly, the American Embassy in Saigon. Thirteen of the South's sixteen provincial capitals were invaded. The worst fighting occurred in the city of Hué, which the Communists held for twenty-five days. American and South Vietnamese soldiers beat back the invasion. In conventional terms, Tet was a victory for South Vietnam and the Americans. That was not the way the world and the United States saw the event. After Tet, the consensus on American chances of winning the war ended.

Like President Johnson's "loss" in the March New Hampshire primary later that year, technical victory did not outweigh the expectations of the margin of victory. Many people still believe North Vietnam "won" the Tet Offensive. It did, but not on conventional, battlefield terms. United States and South Vietnamese troops eventually beat back the enemy, but at a heavy cost exacted from the American public's reaction. Americans saw firsthand during Tet the brutal fighting that attended when a relatively small number of dedicated soldiers carefully entrenched themselves in key positions. It took American troops six and one half hours to take back their own embassy (whose security relied on South Vietnamese troops). Mainly the attacks were a disaster for the Americans and South Vietnamese. The North demonstrated that the Americans were vulnerable despite their overwhelming strength and hoped to drive a wedge between American and South Vietnamese forces, weakening their alliance. North Vietnam wanted to show it was possible for the population in the South to rise up against its government. The North also thought the shock of the offensive would force President Johnson to the negotiating table.

Everything changed after Tet. No year in American history since the Civil War was so tumultuous as the events in 1968 that began with the Tet Offensive. Strong supporters of the war began to reassess their commitments. Certainly the coverage of the war changed. Editors and television producers had for years been trying to temper the reports they were getting from their young reporters in the field, who told them a vastly different story than the one coming from official sources. Even Walter Cronkite, that "most trusted man in America" news anchor, turned against the war. Generals could say, and did say, we were winning the war, and we were. Yet Americans saw a different picture each night on television as a fuller picture emerged of a tenacious enemy fighting for his own country, unwilling to give an inch to the would-be conquerors. Even if the generals and civilian advisors correctly portrayed the offensive as a desperate effort, they could not explain away how a small, outnumbered force could mount a vast attack even in the heart of their enemy's capital. The very barometers of "victory" and "defeat" changed that day in Vietnam.

And a decision that Kennedy thought irrevocable, one that agonized him and his advisors for many months, changed, too.

He no longer felt constrained to criticize Johnson's handling of the war. "Are we like the God of the Old Testament that we can decide in Washington, D.C., what cities, what towns, what hamlets in Vietnam are going to be destroyed?" Kennedy asked during a senate speech in early March. He had become convinced that America needed to withdraw from the war and without delay. Privately, he told an IBM official:

> I'd get out of there in any possible way. I think it's an absolute disaster. I think it's much worse to be there than any of the shame or difficulty that one would engender internationally by moving out. And so, with whatever kind of apologies and with whatever kind of grace I could conjure up, I'd get out of there in six months with all the troops the United States has.[1]

The Tet Offensive changed the course of American history and turned 1968 into a year of inconceivable events.

Vietnam brought out the divided image of Robert Kennedy more than any issue of his time. Critics have charged that the war showed Kennedy at his ruthless, pragmatic worst, that he used the war and the anti-war movement to further his own presidential aspirations. The war was the most important issue of the campaign and its influence could not be ignored. As critical as writers have been about Kennedy's delay in entering the 1968 presidential campaign, that pales in comparison to the political storm an earlier entry would have caused. For he would certainly have been seen as a spoiler, a divider of the Democratic Party. Up until the Tet Offensive, despite widespread protests and opposition to the war, most Americans supported America's involvement in Vietnam and the Johnson administration's policy of bombing North Vietnam.

Bobby Kennedy opposed the war, deeply. Yet every statement he made, his every vote in the senate, was analyzed against his chances in 1968 and/or his relationship with President Johnson. Whether what he said or did actually was about his presidential ambitions or his thoughts about the way Johnson was handling the war, the press headlines focused on 1968. It may not have been the very first of its kind, but the headline the *Houston Chronicle* ran on November 18, 1964 shows how difficult it was for Robert trying to divorce his presidential ambitions from his need to maintain a national profile: "KENNEDY WILL NOT OPPOSE JOHNSON IN '68."[2] Johnson's landslide victory over Senator Barry Goldwater was barely two weeks old when that headline ran. Kennedy could not as much as snip a ceremonial ribbon without it being interpreted as part of his presidential ambition.

America divided against itself after the Tet Offensive. The civil rights movement made clear the divisions that haunted America: white against black, north against south. Vietnam drove wedges dividing college students against the working class, hawks against doves, protesters in the streets of Chicago against that city's police force. If Kennedy seemed divided about his opposition to the war, his indecisiveness lay in finding a practical means to end the war in the years he served as senator. Speaking out more boldly against the war would have driven President Johnson to an even harder position supporting the war. A quick end to the war could not be had by supporting a particular party. Certain Democrats would have ended the war quickly, but they were by no means an anti-war party.

In a similar era of division, a new party formed in the 1850s to oppose slavery, the Republican Party. Politicians declaring themselves Republicans could safely voice opposition to slavery without opposing members of their own party, dividing their electoral strength and thereby aiding the opposing party.

American politicians in the 1960s could not have formed an anti-war party without becoming insignificant. They could only work within existing parties, whether Democratic or Republican, if they wished to succeed in ending the war. Neither party could be identified as being more opposed to the war. The only way Kennedy could have addressed his anti-war position freely would have been outside the party, as a "third-party" candidate, an immeasurably unsound choice. Only by remaining in the Democratic Party, publicly tempering his opposition to it, did Kennedy have any chance of shortening the war.

Five years after Robert Kennedy entered the race for president, the last American troops left Vietnam, four years after Richard Nixon became president. It is hard to see what those years America stayed in Vietnam did for freedom, to protect America's position among nations or to dispel the dissension that bloodied our country's streets. Even without counting the waste of humanity before 1969, the deaths and twisted bodies of the hundreds of thousands in Southeast Asia after that year should serve as condemnation to those whose political aims lack moral authority.

Of all the presidential candidates in 1968 who had a chance of winning, Robert Kennedy had the best chance of ending the war quickly. President Johnson said those who opposed the war would not have been so easily critical if they could sit in his place, face the generals and advisors he had to confront everyday, and then tell them the war should be ended. He was right. Any president could technically end the war with a "stroke of a pen," but the political effectiveness of that leader would have immediately ended. Johnson could not risk destroying his presidency, one that tried to do so much in the areas of civil rights and helping the poor. He wanted to know how another politician would have ended the war without bankrupting his own political currency and that of his party. Johnson forgot that

Robert Kennedy had been there, as close as one could get without sitting in the seat of power himself.

He probably did not want to admit that Kennedy had been the pivotal player in convincing the military to support a Cuban blockade at a time when no one supported any strategy except bombing Soviet missile bases there. Robert understood the need to bring the Joint Chiefs of Staff around to his position and more importantly how to do it. Kennedy had a legitimate claim to being the only candidate with the political wherewithal to end the war.

Robert Kennedy took the plunge to run for president to end the war in Vietnam. Had the political ambition in him been purer, he would have bided his time, entered a political campaign that would have been less divisive and provided a better chance for personal success. He would have run for president anyway, but not at such a precarious time. The safe road was not taken. Instead, he took a riskier path.

Ambition brought him to the edge, but the final leap into the presidential pool came from his deep moral essence. His father's pragmatic drive led him to seek a career in public service, when he could have been, as he once said himself after a particularly trying community meeting, "smoking cigars in Palm Beach." His mother's spiritual training kept him from embracing only worldly ambition. Worldly purpose fused with religious values in Bobby's case, giving us a politician who would rise above the political give and take, the balancing act among competing interest groups, to take a moral stance when America needed more than the advice Cold War tacticians could supply.

Many powerful men resented Robert Kennedy's presence in the corridors of power. They thought themselves smarter and better equipped to lead the United States with their geopolitical hubris. Kennedy shared their conceit at one point. He thought the hearts and minds of nations could be bent toward American will covertly through international sabotage and possibly through more dastardly means. That was his greatest mistake. He could learn from mistakes though, change policies and positions when the ones in place proved inadequate or unworkable. Many others could not. Vietnam had Peloponnesian War consequences for America. Only a few men who had a real chance to rule opposed America's reckless war policy. It is to Kennedy's eternal credit that he stood among them.

Juan Romero was a busboy in the Los Angeles Ambassador Hotel in 1968. He was in the kitchen on June 5, the night Robert Kennedy won the California primary. Romero came from Mexico as a ten-year-old boy. It took a deal with another busboy, sharing tips and picking up the other worker's trays, but he wanted to answer the senator's room service call. He remembered shaking Bobby's hand the day before:

> It was a strong handshake, reassuring and genuine. At that moment, nobody could tell me I was just a busboy, or just a Mexican . . . I felt like I was as American as apple pie.[3]

One more unforeseen event occurred during Robert Kennedy's campaign for the presidency. Bobby had just acknowledged his win in the California primary in the ballroom of the Ambassador. The candidate took a short-cut out through the kitchen. Romero was there waiting for a chance to shake Bobby's hand again. He reached through the crowd for another handshake, never seeing the gun. Then suddenly, the young busboy was holding the bleeding head of Robert Kennedy, who lay sprawled out on the kitchen floor mortally wounded. Sirhan Bishira Sirhan had been waiting, too. Kennedy remained alive until June 6. Bobby's heart continued to beat but the doctors could not repair the damage the bullets had done to his brain.

His body was taken to St. Patrick's Cathedral in New York City. Hundreds of thousands of people gathered in the streets. A special funeral train took his body to Washington D.C. where Robert Kennedy was buried, in Arlington National Cemetery near his brother.

The what ifs or what could have beens never really count. With every such tragedy we are reminded that the corporeal charm of our existence matters little; we instead should cling to lasting purposes, the ideas and dreams that motivate the flesh to achieve something more than the passing of trinkets from generation to generation.

Robert Kennedy did not fear death as maybe he should have because he sensed our individual passing meant little to the progress of humanity. He chose to throw himself into the fray because simple existence did not satisfy his restless soul. Before the artilleries of time remove those who remember Robert Kennedy, we can use his example to transform the awful cynicism of our current political climate. America has always been able to produce people ready to step up and face severe challenges. We can only hope leaders like Robert Kennedy can inspire those we will need when that call comes again.

ACKNOWLEDGEMENTS

Few human endeavors can be completed within the confines of a single human soul. Only the romantic among us thinks the writer toils alone. Every book is the result of an ad hoc collection of support from true believers to whip-cracking keepers of the deadline.

Foremost among the former category has been the editor of the Lives and Legacies series Barbara Leah Ellis. It was she who initiated the idea that an unknown, unpublished book author could tackle this subject. Nothing I have accomplished would have been been possible without her belief and hard work. She's pretty good at cracking the whip, too.

Crossroad's publisher Gwendolin Herder gets my lifelong thanks for taking a chance with this unknown author. Every writer needs an opportunity and a forum; both have Gwendolin and Crossroad provided. Matthew Laughlin of Crossroad is the chief reason this book got out on time and much thanks to him for last-minute dispensation that allowed time for a final push to get this book completed.

Everyone who values historical research should be as well-served as I at the John F. Kennedy Library and Museum. June Payne and the research staff could not have been more courteous and prompt. Allan B. Goodrich, supervisory archivist, and James B. Hill, both of whom work in the audiovisual archives of the library, made my neophyte experience with photo research a pleasant and fruitful one.

I also need to thank Anthony Lewis of *The New York Times* and Daniel Schorr of *National Public Radio* for answering, despite their busy schedules, my desperate plea for help.

Finally, my mother Elizabeth, brother Michael and sister-in-law Maryann deserve apologies for the calls and emails that went unanswered. (At least you can see, with the publication of this book, where I've been.)

CHRONOLOGY

1925 Nov. 20: RFK born, Brookline, Massachusetts
1926 Spring: Family moves to New York

1928 Apr. 4: Ethel Skakel born

1938 Joseph P. Kennedy Sr. appointed ambassador to
      England, family moves to London

1940 Fall: RFK leaves Episcopal St. Paul's School to Catholic
      Portsmouth
      Oct. 23: Joe Sr. resigns as ambassador, returns home

1942 RFK transfers to Milton Academy
1943 Sept.: RFK enters Harvard
1944 Sister Kathleen marries Marquis of Hartington
      Aug. 2: Joseph P. Kennedy Jr. dies flying a secret mission
      over English Channel
      Nov. 1: RFK reports to Lewiston, Maine for Navy training

1946 Feb. 1: RFK assigned to active duty aboard the destroyer
      Joseph P. Kennedy Jr. (named for his dead brother)
      May 30: RFK discharged from Navy
      Summer: Travels to South America with LeMoyne Billings
      Sept.: RFK returns to Harvard

1948 RFK travels to Israel working for the *Boston Post*
      May 14: Kathleen Kennedy Hartington killed in plane
      crash in France
      Sept. 1: RFK enters University of Virginia Law School
1950 RFK marries Ethel Skakel at Greenwich, Connecticut

1925 July 24: John T. Scopes found guilty of teaching evolution

1926 March 16: Dr. Robert H. Goddard demonstrated practicality of rockets at Auburn, Mass. with first liquid fuel rocket

1929 Oct. 29: Stock market crash; begins worst U.S. depression

1939 Hitler invades Poland

1940 Richard Wright's *Native Son* published
May: British and French troops evacuated from Dunkirk
June: Battle of Britain begins

1941 Dec. 7: Japan attacks Pearl Harbor, U.S. declares war on Japan the next day, on Germany and Italy four days later

1942 June 4: Battle of Midway begins, Japan's first major defeat

1944 June 6: Allies invade Normandy

1945 May 7: Germany surrenders
Aug.: Atomic bombs dropped on Japan
Aug. 14: Japan agrees to surrender

1947 June 20: President Truman vetoes Taft-Hartley Labor Act
June 5: Marshall Plan for aid to Europe begun

1948 May 14: Israel declared independent state

1950 June 27: President Truman orders armed forces into Korea
Nov. 1: Two Puerto Rican nationals attempt to kill Truman

1951 RFK graduates from University of Virginia Law School
      July 4: Kathleen Hartington Kennedy born
      Summer: RFK joins Department of Justice, Brooklyn, N.Y.
      Fall: Takes world trip with sister Pat and JFK; latter
          nearly dies in hospital in Japan
1952 Spring: RFK agrees to manage JFK's campaign for senate
      Sept. 24: Joseph Patrick Kennedy III born
1953 Jan.: RFK joins Senator McCarthy's Permanent Investi-
          gations Subcommittee
      July: RFK resigns from McCarthy committee
      Aug.: RFK joins Hoover Commission
      Sept. 12: JFK marries Jacqueline Bouvier
1954 Jan. 17: Robert Francis Kennedy Jr. born
      Feb.: RFK rejoins McCarthy committee as minority counsel
1955 June 15: David Anthony Kennedy born
      Summer: RFK travels to Soviet Central Asia with
          Supreme Court Justice William O. Douglas
1956 Sept. 9: Mary Courtney Kennedy born
      Sept. 12: RFK begins investigations of labor unions
          under the Permanent Investigation Subcommittee
1957 RFK serves as godfather to JFK's daughter Caroline
1958 Feb. 27: Michael LeMoyne Kennedy born
1959 Sept. 8: Mary Kerry Kennedy born
      Sept. 10: RFK resigns from senate subcommittee
1960 RFK begins work on JFK campaign for president
1961 RFK appointed attorney general
      May: RFK gives Law Day speech at University of Georgia
          where two black students enrolled under federal court order
      May 21: RFK orders 500 U.S. marshals into Montgomery,
          Ala. following attacks on Freedom Riders
      Sept. 22: RFK orders Interstate Commerce Commission
          to issue regulations ending segregation in interstate
          bus terminals
1962 Feb.: RFK and Ethel begin "goodwill tour" of the world

1951 J.D. Salinger's *Catcher in the Rye* published
 March 29: Julius and Ethel Rosenberg found guilty of
 conspiring to commit wartime espionage
 Sept. 4: First transcontinental television broadcast, from
 Japanese Treaty Conference, San Francisco
1952 Nov. 1: First hydrogen device explosion at Eniwetok
 Atoll, in the Pacific
1953 Jan. 20: Dwight David Eisenhower inaugurated president
 March 5: Joseph Stalin dies
 May 8: President Eisenhower announces U.S. had given
 France $60 million for Indochina War

1954 Dec.: Senator Joseph McCarthy censured by senate

1955 Feb. 12: U.S. agrees to help train South Vietnamese army
 Dec. 1: Rosa Parks refuses to give up her bus seat in
 Montgomery, Ala.
1956 Sept. 25: First international telephone cable begins operation
 Nov.: John Kennedy elected to senate from Massachusetts

1957 March 13: Teamster leader Jimmy Hoffa arrested
 Nov. 14: Police raid meeting of organized gangsters in
 Appalachia, New York

1960 Nov.: John Kennedy elected president
1961 Jan. 3: U.S. breaks diplomatic relations with Cuba
 April 17: Bay of Pigs invasion of Cuba begins
 April 12: Yuri Gagarin, cosmonaut, becomes first man to
 fly in space and orbit earth
 May 5: Astronaut Alan Shepard, Jr. makes first U.S.
 manned spaceflight
 May 14: Freedom Riders attacked in Anniston, Ala.
 Oct. 27: Russian and American tanks face each other in Berlin
1962 Oct. 1: James Meredith become first black student to
 enroll in University of Mississippi; federal troops
 called in to quell riots that results in two death

Oct. 23: RFK meets with Soviet Ambassador Anatoly
Dobrynin to discuss its nuclear missiles in Cuba

1963 May 24: RFK excoriated by black leaders in NYC meeting
July 4: Christopher George Kennedy born
Aug. 7: JFK and Jackie's son, Patrick Bouvier, dies
Dec. 4: RFK returns to work

1964 June 19: EMK nearly killed in plane crash
Aug. 25: RFK announces candidacy for senate from N.Y.
Nov.: RFK elected to U.S. Senate
1965 Jan.: RFK sworn into senate
Jan. 11: Matthew Maxwell Taylor Kennedy born
March: RFK climbs Mt. Kennedy in Canadian Yukon
1966 June: RFK and Ethel travel to South Africa

1967 March 24: Douglas Harriman Kennedy born
April 25: RFK attacks President Johnson's Vietnam War
Policy

1968 Jan. 30: RFK announces at a meeting of the National
Press Club he will not oppose President Johnson's
reelection under any "foreseeable" circumstances
March 16: RFK announces candidacy for presidency
May 7: RFK wins Indiana primary
May 15: RFK wins Nebraska primary
May 28: RFK loses Oregon primary to Sen. McCarthy
June 4: RFK wins North Dakota and California primaries
June 5: RFK shot in the early morning hours in the the
kitchen of the Ambassador Hotel after announcing
primary victories
June 6: RFK dies from wounds sustained in shooting
June 8: RFK buried in Arlington Cemetery
Dec. 12: Rory Elizabeth Katherine Kennedy born

Oct. 16: JFK shown evidence of missile bases in Cuba

Oct. 28: Soviets agree to remove missiles from Cuba; U.S. agrees to remove NATO missiles in Turkey at a later date

Dec. 24: 1,113 prisoners from Bay of Pigs invasion released by Cuba

1963 June 10: two black students enroll in University of Alabama

Aug. 28: the Rev. Martin Luther King Jr. gives "I Have a Dream" speech during march on Washington, D.C.

Nov. 1: South Vietnamese President Diem assassinated

Nov. 22: JFK assassinated

1964 July 2: President Johnson succeeds in passing civil rights bill

Aug. 7: Congress passes Gulf of Tonkin Resolution

Sept. 27: Warren Commission releases report

1965 Summer: Rev. King organizes march from Selina to Montgomery, Ala. to demand voting rights for blacks

1966 June 29: U.S. begins bombing of Hanoi, North Vietnam

July 1: Medicare begins

1967 June 23: President Johnson meets with Soviet Premier Kosygin in Glassboro, N.J.

Nov. 30: Senator Eugene McCarthy announces candidacy for Democratic nomination for president

1968 Jan. 30: Tet Offensive begins

March 12: McCarthy nearly wins New Hampshire primary

March 31: President Johnson announces withdrawal from election, orders a halt to air and naval bombing in Vietnam

April 4: Rev. Martin Luther King Jr. assassinated

May 10: Vietnam War peace talks begin in Paris

Nov.: Richard M. Nixon elected president

NOTES

Chapter 1: Man of Myths

1. Schlesinger, Robert *Kennedy and His Times*, p. 856.
2. Stein, *American Journey*, p. 196.

Chapter 2: Enfant Terrible

1. Steel, *In Love with Night*, p. 125.
2. David, *Bobby Kennedy*, p. 105.
3. Kennedy, *Times to Remember*, pp. 102–103.
4. Whalen, *Founding Father*, p. 59.
5. Sidney, *The Kennedy Circle*, pp. 190–91.
6. David, *Bobby Kennedy*, p. 30.
7. Ibid., p. 26.
8. Ibid., p. 13.
9. Ibid., p. 17.
10. Schlesinger, *Robert Kennedy and His Times*, p. 126 and *Kennedy Diary*, p. 98.
11. Stein, *American Journey*, p. 50.
12. Ibid., p. 196.
13. Schlesinger, *Robert Kennedy and His Times*, pp. 101–103.
14. Kennedy, *The Enemy Within*, p. 307

Chapter 3: A Splendid Ruthlessness

1. O'Donnell, *"Johnny We Hardly Knew Ye,"* pp. 84–85.

2. David, *Bobby Kennedy*, pp. 62–63.
3. Goodwin, *The Fitzgeralds and the Kennedys*, p. 71.
4. O'Donnell, *"Johnny We Hardly Knew Ye,"* p. 84.
5. Guthman, *Robert Kennedy In His Own Words*, p. 441.
6. Laing, *Robert Kennedy*, p. 93.
7. Hilty, *Robert Kennedy Brother Protector*, p. 47.
8. Stein, *American Journey*, p. 42.
9. Hersh, *The Dark Side of Camelot*, pp. 278–279.
10. Kinnard, *Certain Trumpet*, p. 62.
11. *McCarthy, The Kennedys*, p. 291.
12. Taylor, *The Sword and the Pen*, p. 244.
13. Kennedy, *The Enemy Within*, pp. 249–250.
14. Ibid., p. 251.
15. Brother, *Hilty, Robert Kennedy Brother Protector*, p. 142.
16. Roberts, *Robert Francis Kennedy: Biography of a Compulsive Politician*, p. 110.
17. Laing, *Robert Kennedy*, p. 12.
18. Ibid., pp. 1–3.
19. Shannon, *Heir Apparent*, p. 50.
20. Collier, *The Kennedys*, p. 227.

Chapter 4: Terrible Honesty

1. Kennedy, *Enemy Within*, pp. 313–315.
2. Ibid., pp. 313–315.
3. White, *The Kennedys and Cuba*, pp. 81–84.
4. Hilty, *Robert Kennedy Brother Protector*, p. 425.

Chapter 5: Demagogue

1. Laing, *Robert Kennedy*, p. 76.
2. Schlesinger, *Robert Kennedy and His Times*, p. 815.
3. Mahoney, *Sons & Brothers*, pp. 306–307.
4. Laing, *Robert Kennedy*, pp. 235–236.
5. Ibid., pp. 218–219.
6. Ibid., *Robert Kennedy*, p. 216.

7. Spoto, *Marilyn Monroe: The Biography*, pp. 560–563.
8. Steel, *In Love with Night*, pp. 69–70.

CHAPTER 6: THE ALTAR BOY

1. Collier, *The Kennedys*, p. 325.
2. Sorensen, *The Kennedy Legacy*, pp. 27–28.
3. Laing, *Robert Kennedy*, p. 77.
4. David, *Bobby Kennedy*, pp. 28–29.
5. Ibid., pp. 26–29.
6. Kennedy, *Times to Remember*, p. 162.
7. Ibid., pp. 82–83.
8. David, *Bobby Kennedy*, p. 22.
9. Ibid., pp. 23.
10. Schlesinger, *Robert Kennedy and His Times*, p. 7.
11. David, *Bobby Kennedy*, p. 23.
12. Ibid., pp. 33–34.
13. Schlesinger, *Robert Kennedy and His Times*, p. 44.
14. Sidney, *The Kennedy Circle*, pp. 195–196.
15. Stein, *American Journey*, p. 147.
16. Guthman, *Robert Kennedy In His Own Words*, p. 327.
17. Hennesey, *American Catholic*, p. 235.
18. Schlesinger, *Robert Kennedy and His Times*, p. 191.

iCHAPTER 7: PRESIDENT ONE AND A HALF

1. Guthman, *Robert Kennedy In His Own Words*, pp. 246–258.
2. Ibid., p. 12–13.
3. Reeves, *Profile of Power*, p. 105.
4. Guthman, *Robert Kennedy In His Own Words*, pp. 317–318.
5. Schlesinger, *Robert Kennedy and His Times*, pp. 532–532.
6. Ibid., p. 535.
7. O'Donnell, *"Johnny We Hardly Knew Ye,"* pp. 274–276.
8. Hilty, *Sons and Brothers*, p. 202.

9. Kennedy, *Thirteen Days*, pp. 38–39.
10. *Cold War International History Project Bulletin: Issue 5*, pp. 79–80.

CHAPTER 8: JUSTICE FOR SOME

1. Schlesinger, *Robert Kennedy and His Times*, p. 233.
2. Laing, *Robert Kennedy* pp. 1–3.
3. Sullivan, *The Bureau*, pp. 48, 56.
4. Navasky, *Kennedy Justice*, p. 168.
5. Ibid., p. 277.
6. Schlesinger, *Robert Kennedy and His Times*, p. 234.
7. Ibid., pp. 308–309.

CHAPTER 9: GROWING UP

1. Schlesinger, *Robert Kennedy and His Times*, p. 124.
2. David, *Bobby Kennedy*, p. 15.
3. Ibid., p. 48.
4. O'Donnell, *A Common Good*, p. 326.
5. Schlesinger, *Robert Kennedy and His Times*, p. 813.
6. Laing, *Robert Kennedy*, p. 5.
7. Hilty, *Robert Kennedy Brother Protector*, p. 325.
8. Hilty, *Robert Kennedy Brother Protector*, p. 262.
9. Stein, *American Journey*, pp. 154–155.
10. Mahoney, *Sons & Brothers*, p. 153.
11. Hilty, *Robert Kennedy Brother Protector*, p. 97.
12. David, *Bobby Kennedy*, p. 48.
13. vanden Heuvel, *On His Own*, p. 181.
14. Reeves, *Profile of Power*, p. 475.
15. Schlesinger, *Robert Kennedy and His Times*, p. 585.
16. Schlesinger, Robert *Kennedy and His Times*, p. 592.
17. Ibid., pp. 330–335.
18. Laing, *Robert Kennedy*, p. 4.

19. Stein, *American Journey*, p. 305.

20. Schlesinger, *Robert Kennedy and His Times*, p. 909.

CHAPTER 10: MORAL PRAGMATISM

1. Schlesinger, *Robert Kennedy and His Times*, p. 844.

2. vanden Heuvel, *On His Own*, pp. 264.

3. Bailey, Brandon, *Knight Ridder Newspapers*, June 6, 1998.

BIBLIOGRAPHY

Adler, Bill. (ed). *Robert F. Kennedy Wit, The*, New York: Berkeley Publishing Corporation, 1968.

Bradlee, Benjamin C. *Conversation with Kennedy*, New York: WW Norton & Co. Inc., 1975.

Bryce, James. *American Commonwealth, The*, London: Macmillan and Co., 1888.

Catudal, Honré M. *Kennedy and the Berlin Wall Crisis: A Case Study in U.S. Decision Making*, Berlin: Berlin Verlag, 1980.

Collier, Peter, Horowitz, David. *Kennedys, The*, London: Secker & Warburg, 1984.

Dallas, Rita. *Kennedy Case, The*, New York: G.P. Putnam's Sons, 1975.

David, Lester; David, Irene. *Bobby Kennedy: The Making of a Folk Hero*, New York: Dodd, Mead & Co., 1986.

De Toledano, Ralph. *R.F.K. The Man Who Would Be President*, New York: G.P. Putnam's Sons, 1967.

Fenton, John H. *Catholic Vote, The*, New Orleans: Hauser Press, The Galleon Books, 1960.

Fuchs, Lawrence H. *John F. Kennedy and American Catholicism*, New York: Meredith Press, 1967.

Giglio, James N. *Presidency of John F. Kennedy, The*, Lawrence, Kansas: University Press of Kansas, 1991.

Griswold, Erwin N. *Fifth Amendment Today, The: Three Speeches by Erwin N. Griswold*, Cambridge, Mass.: Harvard University Press, 1955.

Goodwin, Doris Kearns. *Fitzgeralds and the Kennedys, The*, New York: Simon and Schuster, 1987.

Guthman, Edwin O.; Shulman, Jeffrey (eds). *Robert Kennedy In His Own Words*, New York: Bantham Press, 1988.

Hennesey, S.J., James. *American Catholics: A History of the Roman Catholic Community in the United States*, New York: Oxford University Press, 1981.

Hersh, Seymour M. *Dark Side of Camelot, The*, Boston: Little, Brown and Company, 1997.

Hilty, James W. *Robert Kennedy Brother Protector*, Philadelphia: Temple University Press, 1997.

Kennedy, Maxwell Taylor (ed). *Make Gentle the Life of this World: The Vision of Robert F. Kennedy*, New York: Harcourt Brace & Company, 1998.

Kennedy, Robert F. *Enemy Within, The*, New York: Da Capo Press, 1994.

———. *Thirteen Days: A Memoir of the Cuban Missile Crisis*, New York: Penguin Group, The, 1969.

———. *To Seek a Newer World*, Garden City, New York: Doubleday & Company, Inc., 1967.

Kennedy, Rose. *Times to Remember*, Garden City, New York: Doubleday & Co., Inc., 1974.

Kinnard, Douglas. *Certain Trumpet, The*, Washington: Brassey's (US), Inc., 1991.

Laing, Margaret. *Robert Kennedy*, London: Macdonald, 1968.

Lasky, Victor. *Robert F. Kennedy: Myth and Man*, New York: Trident Press, 1968.

Manchester, William. *Death of a President, The*, New York: Harper & Row, Publishers, 1967.

———. *Portrait of a President*, Boston: Little, Brown and Co., 1967.

McCarthy, Joe. *Remarkable Kennedys, The*, New York: The Dial Press, 1960.

McTaggeart, Lynne. *Kathleen Kennedy: Her Life and Times*, Garden City, New York: The Dial Press, 1983.

Mollenhoff, Clark R. *New York*, New York: World Publishing Company, The, 1965.

Navasky, Victor S. *Kennedy Justice*, New York: Atheneum, 1971.

Newfield, Jack. *Robert F. Kennedy: A Memoir*, New York: E.P. Dutton & Co., 1969.

O'Donnell, Helen. *Common Good, A: The Friendship of Robert F. Kennedy and Kenneth P. O'Donnell*, New York: William Morrow and Company, Inc., 1998.

O'Donnell, Kenneth P. and David P. Powers with Joe McCarthy. *"Johnny, We Hardly Knew Ye": Memories of John Fitzgerald Kennedy*, Boston: Little, Brown and Company, 1970.

Prendergast, William B. *Catholic Voter in American Politics: The Passing of the Democratic Monolith*, Washington, D.C.: Georgetown University Press, 1999.

Reeves, Richard. *Profile of Power*, New York: Simon & Schuster, 1993.

Roberts, Allen. *Robert Francis Kennedy: Biography of a Compulsive Politician*, Brookline Village, MA: Branden Press Inc., 1984.

Schlesinger Jr., Arthur M. *A Thousand Days: John F. Kennedy in the White House*, Boston: Houghton Mifflin Company, 1965.

———. *Robert Kennedy and His Times*, Boston: Houghton Mifflin Company, 1978.

Senate Hearing. *Hearing Before the Committee on the Judiciary United States Senate Eighty-Seventh Congress*, Washington: U.S. Government Printing Office, 1961.

Shannon, William V. *American Irish, The*, New York: The Macmillan Company, 1966.

Shesol, Jeff. *Mutual Contempt: Lyndon Johnson, Robert Kennedy, and the Feud that Defined a Decade*, New York: W. W. Norton & Company, 1977.

Sorensen, Theodore C. *Kennedy*, New York: Harper & Row, Publisher, 1965.

————. *Kennedy Legacy, The*, New York: Macmillan Publishing Company, 1969.

Spoto, Donald. *Marilyn Monroe: The Biography*, New York: HarperCollins Publishers, 1993.

Steel, Ronald. *In Love with Night: The American Romance with Robert Kennedy*, New York: Simon & Schuster, 2000.

Stein, Jean. *American Journey: The Times of Robert Kennedy*, New York: Harcourt, Brace Jovanovich, Inc., 1970.

Sullivan, William C. *The Bureau: My Thirty Years in Hoover's FBI*, New York: W.W. Norton & Company, 1979.

Tanzer, L. (ed). *Kennedy Circle, The*, Washington, D.C.: Luce, 1961.

Thompson, Robert E.; Myers, Hortense. *Robert F. Kennedy: The Brother Within*, New York: The Macmillan Company, 1962.

U.S. Congress. *Memorial Services in the Congress of the United States and Tributes in Eulogy of Robert Francis Kennedy*, Washington: U.S. Government Printing Office, 1968.

vanden Heuvel, William; Gwirtzman, Milton. *On His Own: Robert F. Kennedy 1964–1968*, Garden City, N.Y.: Doubleday & Company, Inc., 1970.

Whalen, Richard J. *Founding Father, The: The Story of Joseph P. Kennedy*, New York: The New American Library, 1964.

White, Mark J. (ed). *Kennedys and Cuba, The: The Declassified Documentary History*, Chicago: Ivan R. Dee, 1999.

Witcover, Jules. *85 Days: The Last Campaign of Robert Kennedy*, New York: G.P. Putnam's Sons, 1969.

Wyden, Peter. *Wall: The Inside Story of Divided Berlin*, New York: Simon and Schuster, 1989.

INDEX

189

921
Ken

Sidorenko,
  Konstantin,
  1956-

Robert F. Kennedy.

DATE			